Secrets to Getting a Federal Government Job

By James R. Lint and Dr. Anna H. Lint

Copyright 2017

D1711064

A Hiring Freeze Is Your Time To Improve Your Application And Read This Book!

I hope you will freak out. The new president implemented a hiring freeze! If you panic and say you will stop attempting to work in the federal government, this is good. It is good because you do not have perseverance, which means you will not be a good federal employee. It is good because my friends who do want to work for their country will have less competition. It is good for the hiring manager because the people who freak out are also the people who are just looking for the money and not wanting to work for the government and their nation.

The hiring freeze makes new opportunities for hiring applicants. Time to reassess your strategy to be hired.

When the hiring freeze is lifted, the probability is that the rule will allow managers to hire one person for every two vacancies in their office. This will make it more difficult to be hired and the competition will be at an increased level.

The Manager's View

Look at it from the hiring manager's view is smart throughout your career. Hiring managers will be very eager to hire. (I was a hiring manager during the hiring freeze in 2012-13.) Managers must accomplish the organization mission. It currently has been taking almost six months for a manager to start a hiring action, until there is a warm chair. We have had vacancies and people are asked to share the tasks of the vacant position. When we get a new employee, the people who are handling the increased task will be able to better focus on their own job.

Exceptions

Experienced federal professionals know that every rule and regulation has exceptions. The following are exceptions listed in paragraph #3 the Memorandum: Federal Civilian Hiring Freeze Guidance, dated 31 January 2017 by The White House:

3g. Federal civilian personnel hires made by the Office of the Director of National Intelligence (ODNI) and the Central Intelligence Agency (CIA).

3h. Appointments made under the Pathways Internship and Presidential Management Fellows programs (this does not include the Recent Graduates program). Agencies should ensure that such hires understand the provisional nature of these appointments and that conversion is not guaranteed.

3i. Conversions in the ordinary course to the competitive service of current agency employees serving in positions with conversion authority, such as Veteran's Recruitment Act (VRA) and Pathways programs.

3r. The head of any agency may exempt any positions that it deems necessary to: Meet national security (including foreign relations) responsibilities, or public safety responsibilities (including essential activities to the extent that they protect life and property).

Cyber Is a Critical Need and Has Many Exemptions

Many cyber jobs are located in Intelligence organizations, and considered health and safety. (Think hospital records at military and VA.) Cyber defense jobs are supporting foreign affairs organizations. Cyber organizations are hiring younger employees fresh out of college and veterans. Note most of these exemptions have lots of room for hiring cyber defenders.

Opportunities are available.

There are many areas still hiring under the exemptions. This freeze is only for 90 days. There are opportunities for those job seekers.

There are vacant job positions. There are people doing double work because of those vacancies. People are waiting for you to be hired! Persistence is required in life and government work.

Government work is not always easy. We are supporting our nation. Keep focused on your goals.

A Hiring Freeze Is Your Time To Improve Your Application And Read This Book!

Table of Contents

Introduction and Why

Thank you for taking the first step to getting a Federal Government Job in the US Federal Civil Service.

I am personally glad you are doing this. The federal government has personnel retiring every year. I recently retired. I hope one of you will replace my friends and I as we move on, leaving vacancies for you. We are now exploring the retirement life after Civil Service. While the good that comes at the end of a 36-year career is interesting, it will be for another book. This book has the focus of getting the retirees replaced, and getting YOU a federal job.

Employment in the Federal Government can be unique and interesting. You can play a part working vital interesting issues from Homeland Security, fixing the problems of the homeless, and working in federal organizations like Health and Human Services, FBI, CIA, or military intelligence.

It is not easy to get a federal civil service job. It should not be easy. It should be selective and it should be focused on hiring the best employee. Civil Service is not a job to do well and make a profit. The people in Civil Service work for a higher level reason and that is for the good of the United States of America.

In the first week of President Trump's administration, he created a hiring freeze of the federal workforce. He exempted the military. The Defense Department website reminds us "The Department of Defense employs more than 700,000 civilians in an array of critical positions worldwide, with opportunities for people from all walks of life. If a competitive salary, great benefits, unsurpassed training, and the pride of defending our nation interests you, then find your future with us." There are plenty of jobs in Department of Defense. They also have many that are entry and intern training positions.

I did work in Civil Service and the military. I started as a 17-year-old Private in the US Marine Corps, with a GED. I ended as a GS-15, the highest manager grade level, which is equal to a colonel in the Military and I have a Master's degree in Business Administration. I also have plenty of government training in Counterintelligence, Security, Intelligence, and management. While people talk about the cost of education in college, those employed in US federal civil service have no debt education. I had military tuition assistance, veteran benefits, and US federal civil service training and professional development courses. I went from a GED to an MBA with no education debt. There are growth opportunities, and I am living proof. I believe you can also.

Federal government work is interesting and can take you to the highest levels of the US government. You will have an opportunity to share your skills for the nation and often serve in other locations where your skills are needed. (Civil Service will pay your moving cost, and they are very generous.)

I have different views on the hiring process having been an employee that applied and was hired in many different jobs, in both the US and overseas. Additionally, as I went up to more senior positions, I became a hiring manager. If you would have applied for my organization, I would have been the one reading your resume, interviewing you, and approving the final hiring decision. I have seen hiring from both sides and that will be the basis of the information in this book.

I have created a general advertising Facebook page about the book and it is posted in the Epilog, at the end of the book. This may be used for conversations about job hunting. I will create a second Facebook site that will allow you to ask questions about the hiring process and getting a federal civil service job. (I will continue the discussion started in this book about, "Should I Send an Introduction Letter to a Federal Hiring Manager? -- Three reasons I say HECK NO." This could keep you out of jail and out of the eye of upset hiring managers. I have created one public site and one private group and those people who have bought the book will have a way to enter that group through the answer of a question about the book. (The question may be what is the 5th letter in the 3rd chapter.) You will have a resource to get any questions not answered in this book, successfully answered for your career search. I hope to invite a friend who is a Civilian Personnel Office administrator. She is currently in the system and deals with every day hiring problems.

There is NO promise of a job just because you buy this book. You must research job announcements for your job. We will give you some details and methods; you have to create a good resume for the job you desire. Your competition is going to be good. You have to evaluate your skills against the job vacancy.

All profits and proceeds from the book will go to the Lint Center for National Security Studies where we give scholarships for people looking to grow in the national security field. See connect to the Center for scholarships and volunteering opportunities.

The PROs of Working for the Government

Government work is rewarding with a competitive salary that is based on the "cost of living" in that location. This is also called locality pay. The cost of living in Washington DC or New York City differs between the cost in Gladstone, Missouri or in a location in North Dakota. Civil Service pays based on the differences of where you live, which keeps us from moving to a place where we might be shocked by the cost of living.

Benefits

A career with the US government provides employees with a comprehensive benefits package. As a federal employee you and your family will have a wide range of benefits that are designed to make your career rewarding. Eligibility for some benefits are dependent on the type of position you hold whether it is full-time or part-time work. Also, the benefits are different if you are overseas or in an area where you cannot get certain normal American comforts. An example would be when I lived in Korea, as a civilian. Because housing is different in Korea than in America, the government provided me with either quarters on post or an off post apartment. What an opportunity to be able to live in a foreign country and a foreign culture. The benefits for being able to live overseas while still maintaining access to American goods through the PX and commissary are wonderful. Sometimes when you are living overseas in an area without US military forces, there will be no PX or commissary.

Healthcare is an issue for most Americans, but in civil service, it is not an issue. Civil servants have a plethora of health care options. Those options will cover health, dental, vision, long-term care insurance plus the flexible spending account (FSA).

Salary is Public Knowledge

In many companies, your salary is very private. In all my life in federal service, in both military and civil service, my salary has been available for anybody to see because it is public record. A private makes X amount depending on the number of years of service he has. In addition, civil service while we do not have ranks like the military, we do have grades. Grades have a pay chart; and it is broken down by years of service and your grade. There are some special charts beyond the normal general schedule (GS). The Law Enforcement Officer (LEO) pay charts take into the account the long and extra hours that law enforcement may be required to perform. There is also a Federal Wage System (FWS) that is for what is commonly referred to as blue-collar work in the civilian world. These would be people who work in the trades skilled craftsmen and sometimes employed by military depots, the Park Service, and in people who take care of the government fleet of cars. The pay charts may all be found usually by a simple Google of "OPM pay chart 2017 or the year.

Flexible Hours and Telework

Federal civil service has flexible work schedules and telework. Not every job can use these type work schedules. Some jobs will let you telework from home some jobs will not. If your job requires the use of classified material or intelligence material, obviously, you could not do this from your house. Some jobs are required to be at a government workplace and telework. Some jobs can work nine hour days for two weeks and you get one day off out of that two-week period. Normally people work 40-hour work weeks. The time cards are submitted every two weeks. Some people even work 10 hour days and take two days off during the 80 hour pay period. There are jobs in the government that are very flexible. Some jobs are not. If you are briefing and the President of the United States, you have to go to his house not yours. If your FBI agent and there is an investigation, you might not be working out of your house but have to go to the crime scene.

The federal service has a variety of vacation or what we call "leave" programs. There are situations and regulations to cover a variety of emergency leaves, military related leave issues, as well as normal leave. Do not worry, civil-service has all of this written down and is easy to find. When you get hired, this will all be briefed to you.

Training and Professional Development

One of the greatest benefits and federal civil service is the professional development programs. Every organization and agency has their own professional development programs and some are better than others. The federal government has intern programs that last two years with fully paid training and travel funds for you to travel to different places for the best training. I was involved in both intern programs for intelligence and security. And they were allowed to travel to the best government schools across the country for a variety of different courses some of the week or two, and some longer. At the manager level, I attended a cohort program that came to my installation where the instructors would teach a few days each month for over a period of a year. There they discussed education at the MBA level. They were teaching managers to become executives. It was a great program and the price was wonderful. You see when you were a civil service employee, you are paid to attend these courses. The opportunities are fantastic.

Travel

Frequently overlooked areas are worldwide travel, the adventure, and the ability to make a difference. Civil service employees are not focused on making a profit for a company, but maintaining, improving, and taking care of Americans and often allies. To do that, we have a chance to travel to make a difference, while not taking an unpaid sabbatical to travel around the world. We travel, have an adventure, and stay financially solvent. You cannot get a better job than one that have fun and adventure.

Some of The Bad Parts of Working in The Government

When I joined the Marine Corps in 1975, the slogan was "We don't promise you a rose garden" and some said that was so true. Or the politically incorrect would say that they did promise you the fertilizer. But in that work in the Marine Corps, I had so much training and learned so much. Not that I was smart enough to realize at the time. Most of the rest of the US federal government civil service will not be as bad. (Some are thinking this is good news.)

Paperwork

Many people say that bureaucracy is horrible. Many people will say that bureaucracy is what makes civil service horrible or hard to work with. What people fail to understand is that bureaucracy is nothing but a system. As hackers will tell you, a system has capabilities and the ability to overcome and make it your own. The same goes for bureaucracy.

Bureaucracies tell you how to do something. Bureaucracies tell you exactly how it must be done. Bureaucracies have lots of regulations that tell you what you need to do. Those that do not read the regulations - fail. Those that read the regulations, learn the regulations, and apply the regulations will win. If you turn it around and look at it bureaucracies tell you exactly what they want. Paperwork is now computerized. Paperwork and bureaucracies are easy to overcome and make them work for yourself.

Imagine if your parents did not teach you how to cross. Cars move back and forth. Cars are big. But, learning how to use a crosswalk or even a crosswalk with a stoplight takes the challenge out of crossing the street.

Paperwork must be done to request a vacation. A bureaucracy will tell you which form and how to fill out that form to be able to go on your vacation. When you look at it that way, doesn't a bureaucracy seem good and easy?

The Hiring Process – Overview

Federal civil service has a long recruitment process. It is fair and it has integrity. Isn't that what you would want in the hiring process? There are many checks and balances. The process is getting faster, but it still maintains the safeguards. The federal civil service is built to give everyone an equal chance to be hired.

Some people attacked the hiring process as tough, especially when they see the variety of jobs that are available. If you do not know what job series, career field, or type of work you are aiming for, the hiring process will be difficult. If you apply for jobs that you are not qualified for, you will not get hired. You have to look for jobs and jobs in the grades that you qualify for to get hired.

Go to **"USAJOBS"** and search for the jobs you desire. Later, we will explain various jobs series and categories to help you find a government. In USA jobs, you should review the job announcement. Determine if your package has all the information. Update your resume if needed and submit the application. This is not hard!

The first part of the federal hiring process is to create a USAJOBS profile. This is easy by going to www.USAJOBS.gov. The first page tells you how to create USAJOBS profile. In this profile you can upload all of the information that you will need and resume for future jobs. More data will be provided in another chapter on USAJOBS website and resume requirements.

Secret number one is that you never apply for only one job and wait for the answer. I have often told people for the senior jobs that you are not job hunting unless you have 100 resumes submitted. I have always submitted more. I had a successful career doing this.

During my time as a hiring manager in the Washington DC area, I would often be overwhelmed with resumes. I was hiring for intelligence and security specialist. I was located in Aberdeen Proving Ground, Maryland, which is commuting distance to Fort Meade, Maryland. We were also in the Washington DC commuting area. For intelligence and security specialist, I was in a very target rich environment. First, the Civilian Personnel Office would screen the resumes before they would get to me. This was good because they would use a computer screen resumes for keywords. For security specialists protecting classified information, there are key core competencies in this career field. If you are a security guard at Walmart, you would not qualify for a security specialist in the 0080 career field for classified material protection. It was critical that CPO would screen resumes. By the time they were finished screening, they often only had 200 highly qualified resumes left. As I said, this is an area of many 0080 security specialists. Having only 200 resumes was very overwhelming, I had no idea how many were screened out, but 200 resumes is too many for hiring. (Yes, we can get frustrated with the hiring process just as the applicants do!)

When I was hiring in New Jersey for 0080 security specialist, we would often only get less than 10 resumes. Often those resumes were not highly qualified. The reason is simple; New Jersey did not have the concentration of 0080 security specialist. Therefore, we often had to grow our own security specialist. The way we did this was through an excellent intern program, where we would hire people with little experience and a college degree. We would then put them in a two-year, fully funded, training program. I wanted you to understand location matters. The location you are requesting job will also show some of the depth of your competition.

You will not get rich, but you can save for retirement

You will not get rich working in civil service. The job is to help the country. While the government does take care of its people, it is not designed to make you rich. I will say that working federal civil service will make you rich in experience and memories. There are some jobs that are uniquely government. There is nowhere else that will allow you to be a federal investigator (FBI), work on policy that will impact the nation, serve in an embassy overseas representing your country, or even investigating people conducting espionage and working a counterintelligence mission. Those are inherently federal government jobs. These will give you satisfaction that is unique to the federal government. It will not make you rich.

What will make you financially healthy is controlling your spending and planning your savings. The federal government gives its employees an excellent tool to use for this goal. The Thrift Savings Plan (TSP) is a retirement savings and investment plan for federal employees. It offers similar savings and tax benefits that many private companies offer their employees under a 401(k) plans. The TSP is a defined contribution plan. This means that you decide how much to put into your TSP account. Do not complain in later life that you do not have money saved return. Remember you decide how much to put into your TSP. In many places, you will be offered matching funds for up to a specific amount 4% to 5%. A secret for life not a secret for getting hired, but if you do not put in enough funds to receive all of the matching funds you have just given your employer money. You've also taken a pay cut because you did not take advantage of the generous matching funds.

The real advantage of having the opportunity to use the TSP is that it has the lowest cost to fund users which is something you cannot get from commercial mutual funds. Also when you consider the size of the federal workforce who are allowed to put into the TSP, you can see where the investment size of the TSP is large.

Political Appointees – Hard to get, and changing leaders

Another negative of civil service is the fact that political appointees can come and go. Some of them will be your boss or your boss's boss. They will start projects and in four years they will leave. Some will be good some will be less than. But it is just a fact of life be.

Having new bosses and changing the focus and mission and life of an organization can actually be good. It brings new life and activity; it also brings new opportunity. When people move around and new jobs open, there is an opportunity for you to apply. While most of us won't get a political appointee job, they are available. Also, when new bosses are coming there looking for new people to guide, this is again an opportunity for you.

Competitive, there are other good people also

In the last negative we will discuss is that federal civil service is highly competitive. That is good because it will make those who are inside work with better people. That is bad for those trying to get in, because it is competitive. Never think that you will be the number one person for a job vacancy unless you know all the competition throughout the country and those members of federal civil service who may apply from overseas while serving overseas. It is hard to guess what the competition is for a specific job. Never assume you are the only or the best. This leads us to realizing that we need to put in a fantastic resume and application package. It also makes us realize that we must submit more than one resume to get a civil service job.

Just like a lottery, the more tickets you have the more chances you have to win. The more resumes you have about the better you can assess the quality of your resume against other competitors. If you do not get any interviews maybe you are applying for the wrong positions or the wrong grades. Maybe you did not qualify for what you are applying for. Assess and reassess your application, given improvements and see how that works on getting an interview.

Pick a job for the short term, but pick a career for long term enjoyment

Where we start your job hunting depends on where you are in your career path. Some people may be mid career, some people at the beginning of their career. Most things in life are viewed from where you are sitting in life.

First job

If you are at the beginning of life, and you are not independently wealthy, and do not need a job..., You can wait until the perfect job arrives. Be thankful for your situation, most of us are not there. First time job hunters need to worry about getting into the system. They need to worry about getting experience. They need to look at it on the hiring managers view to determine their value to the employer. If you have a degree or no degree but no experience, what do you think the hiring manager sees as your potential. How can he justify a salary for you? To be competitive, you need to look at things from other people and not yours. Often, people think only of themselves, they should be hired because they are hungry. No company will stay in business if that is the only reason they hire employees. You have to bring value to the employer.

For your first job maybe you should look not for your most fun employment, for the best employment to get experience. A lot of the best managers have started at the bottom. They will recognize your drive when you start at the bottom and work your way up. For that first job, look for ANY job, grab it, and gain the experience.

As a former hiring manager, I saw many resumes that were full of academic accomplishments and information. While that is nice, I did not see skills that were employment ready. One hiring manager told me before that if you remember your GPA, the problem is you probably do not have needed experience. Some resumes are packed with various classes attended to make it look like a full-page resume. Remember, hiring managers did not get to their position by being stupid.

Second job

In federal civil service, you are eligible for promotion after 52 weeks in the same position. Let me translate that: You are eligible for a promotion if smart enough to apply for and get it. I am continuously surprised by the people who are high quality and will not apply for new job at 52 weeks. Some people get in that job that they enjoy. Those who were in the military and have a retirement in the getting their first civil service job, this can be understood. Those who complain about their need for a higher salary, this cannot be understood that they would stay in the same position without submitting for new positions. In civil service, you do not get a promotion just based on time and grade and that the sun is shining. YOU have to apply for a position with increasing responsibility, increasing value to the government, and valuing your increased skills.

If you do not apply for position with a higher grade, you will **not** get a promotion. The way to apply is the same way you got your original... Hunt for a new job position. For this, you would go to USAJOBS, review the available job vacancies, and apply for those vacancies. Remember, when you are a GS-07 you can apply for a GS-09, when you are GS-09 you may apply GS-11. Those are two grade increase and many organizations allow that.

Third job

When you are looking for your third job, you may find that you have got the highest job in your job series in that location. If that is the case, remember one thing, America and the world are large places for civil service jobs. It may be time for you to move. Many will say, I cannot move; I have kids in school. The military, civil service, and private companies have moved for years. From the start of my work life until I retired, I made 25 moves. It is possible with a positive bad. Kids adapt and even improve their social skills. "Military Brats" have done this for years...successfully. Spouses have done it for years, also with success. My wife increased her pay and level of work with every move I made. It can be done.

Many government jobs will offer to pay for a government move. They want to keep good people. Some places, it is harder to get to come and there will be more opportunity for a paid move. Some places, a soft skill will be easy to hire locally and they will not go to the expense of paying for move. It depends on the situations, the organization needs, and the budget situation.

Remember, every 52 weeks you are eligible for promotion. I would often apply for new jobs at the 11-month mark. This would allow me to have my 52 weeks by the time that the hiring process.

Questions to consider for your job placement

1) Decide what you want? Do you want a job or career?

2) What job series do you desire? Do you like working outside or inside?

3) Desk or walking? What are your skills?

4) Do you want to work as a manager? Do you have the skills and education?

5) Are you willing to move? Is there a government facility in your area?

6) Do they have your job series? Your desired grade? You have to go where the jobs are located.

7) **INTERNSHIPS**: There are 1 and 2-year intern programs, most require a college degree. These are now called the Pathway Program.

OPM website reports the following: President Obama signed Executive Order 13562, entitled "Recruiting and Hiring Students and Recent Graduates," on December 27, 2010. This Executive order established two new programs and modified another. They are the Internship Program for current students; the Recent Graduates Program for people who have recently graduated from qualifying educational institutions or programs (2 years from the date the graduate completed an academic course of study); and the reinvigorated Presidential Management Fellows (PMF) Program for people who obtained an advanced degree (e.g., graduate or professional degree) within the preceding two years. These programs, collectively the Pathways Programs, are streamlined developmental programs tailored to promote employment opportunities for students and recent graduates in the Federal workforce.

As directed by the Executive order, OPM issued a final Pathways Rule to implement these programs. The final rule aims to improve recruiting efforts, offer clear paths to Federal internships for students from high school through post-graduate school and to careers for recent graduates, and to provide meaningful training and career development opportunities for individuals who are at the beginning of their Federal service.

These internships are available for **two years** after college, unless you were in the military after college and you will have six years to use the Pathways Program.

Federal Application Process for You

The very first part of learning about Federal Application Process is to **create a USAJOBS profile**. This USAJOBS profile will be used throughout your career. Your USAJOBS profile holding your resume, your supporting documentation, transcripts, veteran support documentation, and even information from responding to your resume. In USAJOBS, you will be able to see the employers' responses as they go through the hiring. You will see referrals or decline to refer to the hiring manager. When you are creating your profile, you will have the option to make your resume searchable by hiring managers. This is a good option to take advantage for special skills where they can authorize special hiring authorities. These are often in research and development and some cyber defense positions. In the last 36 years, I have never had a hiring search for resumes and contact me. During the last 6 years when I had hiring authority, I never searched resumes or contacted applicants based on the searches.

Part of the required documentation in the USAJOBS portal is to document any unique experience or federal preferences. In the federal government, there are many different categories of employees and preferences. If you are a former employee, you may be eligible for **merit** promotion. If you are a former employee stationed overseas, you will have *"returned rights"*. Both of these are hiring to help people in the service. Just because you took a job overseas does not mean that the federal civil service will not bring you back home to the US. Additionally, military wives who are overseas accompanying their military spouse have preference for civil service jobs in the area where their spouses located. There are enhanced hiring programs for Peace Corps and AmeriCorps Vista alumni. They have a preference in the federal government for hiring due to their experience in some of the unique jobs of the federal government.

To find a job, you will need to decide which category or job series you are going search. When searching in USAJOBS, you can search multiple categories in job series. There are categories computer science, economists, mathematical statistics, nurses, contracting, finance, auditing, and information technology management. There are often USAJOBS areas that appear like ads or another area is "Explore Opportunities". When you see those you will know that is a critical need for the government. It is easier to get hired based on their "Explore Opportunities" section which is often the result of a new organization or reorganization.

When you find a job, you will be able to use previously uploaded resumes and the documentation mentioned above you will be able to reuse the same documentation and resume for multiple job applications. Often you can put a different cover letter for that job application. You may also upload different versions of your resume to USAJOBS and pick which resume use for that job series. You are limited to five resumes. You could have one resume that is for 0132 job series Intelligence and one resume that would be for 0080 job series which is security specialist. In my case, I was trained for both of these job series as a counterintelligence specialist in the military.

Another interesting feature in USAJOBS is that you may save your searches. You can have up to 10 different searches with multiple job series/MOSs. You can also have the system send you an email with the different search results every day, every week, or every two weeks. Your searches can be of jobs in different locations, in addition to different job series and grade levels.

It is critical that you review the job announcement prepare your application, and then RE-READ the job announcement. It is amazing the number of times people miss items that are required in the job announcement. This can be a reason to disqualify you from this job. (I have seen the same thing as a professor teaching college where students will skip over a part of the assignment.)

In the 1990s to submit the application, you were required to print all of your documents, have an original signature, and find a stamp, package it, and mail it. Having done the old system, I am a real believer in USAJOBS. This website (https://www.usajobs.gov/)is very easy and user-friendly to use.

The bottom line of the **USER** process is to create a USAJOBS profile, search for your jobs, review your job announcement, prepare your application, and submit via the button on USAJOBS website.

USAJOBS is a great website because of the technology advances. If there is anything you learn from this book, it is that you must send out many resumes. It becomes very easy to apply for jobs. It is as easy as clicking one button to apply for another job.

The gold information that you need is that you have to create a profile. Veterans will have an opportunity to also upload their DD 214 and any veteran disability. Often they will have a Veterans Administration (VA) letter stating the level of their disability. This can also be uploaded into the USAJOBS portal. You need to go into USAJOBS's once a year and renew the information, update the information, and recertify your resume. This ensures all of your documentation stays in the portal.

Notice to Applicants: Please ensure you keep copies of all documents you uploaded or faxed, including your resume, as well as any

notifications sent to you. They will be deleted from the system after 3 years of the closing date of the announcement.

When you have successfully submitted your application, you will get something back like the below email:

This is to acknowledge the receipt of the Occupational Questionnaire you submitted for the job vacancy announcement shown above. We will assess your qualifications based upon the responses you provided in the questionnaire, as well as all other materials requested in the vacancy announcement. When this evaluation is completed, you will be notified of the results with another e-mail message.

It is important to note that in many cases submitting the Occupational Questionnaire does NOT complete your application. Most jobs also require the submission of a written application or resume, as well as supporting materials such as transcripts and Veterans Preference documentation.

TO ENSURE THAT YOU RECEIVE CONSIDERATION FOR THIS POSITION, READ AND FOLLOW THE INSTRUCTIONS IN THE VACANCY ANNOUNCEMENT.

Dear James,

Your application status has been updated for the following opportunity(ies) in USAJOBS. To view your updated status, log in to your USAJOBS account.

Control Number: 459437100

Department:	Department of the Army
Agency:	U.S. Army Intelligence and Security Command
Job Title:	Intelligence Specialist (Operations)
Series & Grade:	GG-0132-14
Announcement #:	WTST167376781856333

Our records show that you signed up to be notified when the status of your application for a job you applied to changes. To unsubscribe or update your preferences for USAJOBS notifications, log in to USAJOBS.

Sincerely,

The USAJOBS Team
U.S. Office of Personnel Management
1900 E Street NW. Washington, DC 20415

To make sure you get USAJOBS emails to your inbox (and not your spam) add 'notifications@usajobs.gov' to your address book.

View from A Recent College Graduate and Job Applicant – Chapter Contributed by John Wiseman

The job hunting process is a daunting adventure. However, you have chosen to read this book and therefore have a leg up on those that have not. That is a major theme when applying for Federal Government jobs: How can you get the leg up on the overwhelming competition that exists on the job market? There are people with more education, experience, and time in the field than you do. Especially if you are a recent graduate looking to get your foot in the door. That means each step you take must have meaning and be a definitive step towards whatever job title or agency you wish to end up with. The first step in this process is the most important: understanding what direction you would like to take with your career.

I started thinking about what I wanted to do when I was in high school and therefore was able to enter college knowing what major I wanted and how I wanted to approach my studies. I knew that I wanted to learn more about the international community and especially the Middle East and Africa. I surmised that there would be a large need for employees with knowledge in that area once I graduated and decided I would enter the Federal Government that way. I also knew that having the ability to use multiple languages was necessary to stand out among other applicants. After tinkering with a Rosetta Stone program in high school, I decided to minor in Arabic. During college I also completed research for my Arabic language professor on multiple occasions, giving me more experience. All of this was to build my resume. I honestly wish I had started looking for internships in high school, but hindsight is 20/20. You should always be looking for and taking opportunities that will build you resume in a way that will appeal to your future employers, which brings me to your next step in the process: Who should I work for and in what capacity?

Finding a mentor who could help you answer that question is extremely important. Having someone who is not only knowledgeable about the inner workings of the hiring process but is also experienced in applying for jobs will also give you more of an advantage over the competition. I was lucky enough to have two individuals that met these characteristics and I can say that without either of them helping me along the way I would not have been as successful at both finding and applying for jobs. They assisted me in writing me resume and guided me on which direction my career should go based on my education and interests. They were also able to tell me stories about their time in the government, which also assisted in opening my eyes to what possibilities the government had for me.

Another way to figure out your career path is to use job exploration tools found in many places online much like this one: https://www.intelligencecareers.gov/. This will give you an idea of what job title your skills and desires match up with, as well as with which agencies you should apply to. However, the most important website you will use will be usajobs.gov. Here you will not only find a plethora of job openings, but also search tools that help dissect which path you should take. First, it gives you the opportunity to set up a government style resume which is much more detailed than your run-of-the-mill resume, but that is all laid out for you under the build-your-resume option. Your resume and profile will be one of the first things that a possible employer sees, so it must be your best. Be as detailed as possible in your description of your work duties and make sure you include both paid and volunteer positions. Make sure to include buzzwords that would be easily identifiable if someone were to skim your resume.

It is important that the person who is looking at your resume knows exactly what you have learned and the responsibilities you've taken on at these jobs and how they have prepared you for the job you applied for. While you should put as much information in that effectively communicates who you are and what experience you have, be sure to keep your points concise and meaningful. Be wary that a hiring manager has to read many, many applications and would rather not read more than they have to. Finally, as the CEO of The Lint Center has told me while giving me advice on this topic, do not over sell your abilities. It would be embarrassing for you and extremely frustrating for the employer to find out that you are not the person you have described in your resume. Therefore, make sure the profile you create reflects the experience that you have and promotes your ability to serve the government while also maintaining a humble awareness of your abilities. **Along this same line of thinking is that you should never lie about anything on your application.** This may not only stop you from receiving consideration for the job you applied for but it could also end up derailing any future plans you had with joining the Federal Government. This is most important when completing the Assessment Questionnaires that you will fill out when applying on USAJobs.

USAJobs has a multitude of ways to search for your potential future employer. First, you could just simply type into the search bar and go from there, but I would recommend using the many tools available to you to refine and condense your search. For example, as a Recent Graduate I chose to start most of my searches under the Pathways Recent Graduate Program which has a tab on the home-page of the website. One of the most helpful areas for a Recent Graduate would be the "Federal occupations by college major" tab you find once you have clicked on the Recent Graduate option. This way you are able to single out job vacancies that you might be more interested in based on your educational knowledge. I would also recommend signing up for weekly email blasts from the website containing job vacancies that are most suited to what you are looking for.

I have applied to 80 different jobs on USAjobs and only two have referred me to the hiring managers. Here is the story for one of them. In December of 2015 I applied for a position at the United States Secret Service and did not hear back until June of 2016. When I applied I had completed research on the position as well as the Service itself so I knew what to expect in terms of job requirements. The most surprising thing for me was the time it took to get through the multi-step process of being hired. On one hand you could complain about the length of time it took to get there but on the other hand, and this is the position I have chosen to follow. It is reassuring that the Secret Service takes this much time and effort to vet and make sure that those who are going to be holding a very important security position are both up for the job and the type of person that would exemplify the ideals of a Secret Service employee. That being said, the process for most positions in the Federal government will take a very long time to complete due the background check that will be required. You will have to be very patient.

Sometimes organizations get back-logged with applicants and sometimes job postings are only there because they are required to be publicly posted. Sometimes, there is an internal hire that may get promoted unless, there is an outside applicant that is better than an employee with that experience. Those people will obviously beat you in a skills completion for a specific job. Do not let this frustrate you. Use this as motivation to push you to continue to apply for jobs. Keep checking up on old applications and you will be successful. You will also most likely have to fill out many pages of paperwork. Make sure that you fill these out with as few mistakes as possible. Again, wasting a hiring manager's time with easy fixes is not in your best interest. I had my SUPER interview in November of 2016 where I was told what my responsibilities would be and what kind of time commitment would be needed of me. It was extremely humbling to be in the same room with Special Agents who were so accomplished and held the position that I hope to have one day.

Joining the Federal Government is not easy, but it is definitely a worthwhile aspiration. The job security as well as the potential to continue to climb the corporate ladder is something that makes applying and waiting for employment worth it. But to get there, you must have a desirable background, patience, and preferably a mentor who is there to guide and assist you along the way. Do not lie in any way on your application. Your future employer wants to know exactly who they are hiring and to find the derogatory information during your background check would be detrimental to you getting your dream job.

Author Bio:

John Wiseman is a graduate of Boston University's Pardee School of Global Studies and currently the Executive Officer to the CEO of the Lint Center for National Security Studies. He studied International Relations and Arabic and has aspirations to join the Federal Government.

The Hiring Process from The Hiring Manager's Eyes

In battle, if you think only about your war plan and your way of operating, you improve your chances of *losing*. Remember the enemy gets a vote in the battle and your activity also. Just as in battle, you must look at both sides of an activity, the same should be done in the hiring process. In fact, this is good advice for most interactions in your career. People can separate themselves by viewing the manager as an adversary or learning to think like a manager. Why did the manager do that? In the beginning of our career, we often have no understanding why a manager does something. We think they are crazy. We fail to understand what they are thinking, and often do not even try to think about their thoughts or their process. In Intelligence, we have to think like the enemy, like the friendly's, and determine what operational impacts occur not from the enemy or friendly.

It is often thought that the manager does not make sense... from the view of a person who has not been in those manager's shoes. But, if you had been trained as a manager or had that experience, you would instantly see that there are budget issues, personnel issue, and other impacts in most activities. We know the budget does not grow on a tree, we have not seen the money tree. So maybe we need to look at why the managers are thinking that way.

The start of the process

First, the hiring manager must determine that there is a vacancy. This is easy because often somebody retired or moved to a new job. Then, the manager has to put in a requisition to his boss/manager requesting placement, a modified position, or possibly even a new position. This means the manager has to spend time reviewing the position description, the budget, the manning documents to come up with that analysis on the best way to fill a vacancy in his/her office with the best skill set to improve his mission success.

After his/her manager approves his/her analysis in the direction, he/she desires to move forward, the hiring manager, then, must contact the Civilian Personnel Office (CPO). These are the government human resource or HR specialists. They review the information from the manager's analysis, current vacancy announcements, and any requirements or recent law changes. If there is already a vacancy announcement for the same job series, in the same area, and the duties are close enough, there is a potential to move faster by combining two hiring actions with one vacancy announcement. That vacancy announcement would list two vacancies vice a single vacancy.

The CPO has a library of all past vacancies announcements for 20 or 30 years. Therefore, often the civilian personnel specialist can pull a previous vacancy announcement and make some modification and publish the vacancy announcement quicker. If it is a new position, the hiring manager has to get a new vacancy announcement approved for the recommended grade. This involves many offices and people to ensure that the government paid the right amount of money for the skill set that is required. This can also delay this process for 2 to 3 months and ability to start the hiring action.

When the Civilian Personnel Office specialist gets final approval for the grading of the position (rank/pay), and the vacancy announcement, only then, can the job be finally advertised. The minimum is normally 10 days to 30 days for the vacancy announcement to be published on USAJOBS. There are exceptions to every rule in federal government work. While various governmental departments work differently, this is a good rule of thumb.

The fun begins when the job announcement closing date arrives. As part of the original package requesting of the action from Civilian Personnel Office, the hiring manager had to submit five to seven "Key Words" pertaining to the job vacancy and job position description. These keywords will help computer sort through the resumes and sort by quality. Sometimes, some positions can get a thousand resumes. This helps sort and makes it a manageable event. Remember, while a manager is working the hiring action, he still has his normal job to do. In Maryland, Fort Meade/ Aberdeen area, the civilian personnel office would often refer 150 to 200 qualified resumes to the hiring manager. This was an area with a high concentration of intelligence and security professionals.

Remember, as I said, the hiring manager has other duties than just this hiring action. The first time I received a vacancy announcement results, it was 200 resumes and I was shocked. This shows the criticality of getting the correct keywords to bring up the best resumes. My hiring actions for intelligence and security job series in New Jersey would often only result in 10 resumes. Maryland would give an overwhelming choice of resumes. And truly, it is overwhelming for hiring manager to need to review 100+ resumes each of them can be four pages long with multiple attachments and documentation in addition to a cover letter.

Think of seeing this pile of resumes is the paper copies in the old days or virtually in your computer. How would you feel to see this and know that you might want to go home in the next few days. This is an overwhelming portion of the job that is in addition to the normal workload. You cannot read each one of these and remember the specifics and make a selection. Two reasons this is true. One, nobody's memory is that good. Two, legal reasons. The process must be documented so that if there is a complaint later on the hiring manager may show how he/she determined the winning selection. So hiring managers have to make a matrix to chart out your resume review.

Your resume sorting matrix must show selective areas that differentiate the various candidates' capability. So, we have seen that the hiring manager has had to put in a request for a newly vacant job, then he has had to get approval from his manager, work with the civilian personnel office to get the vacancy announcement put out to the public, and then sort resumes. And you thought, life as a manager was easy! (Smile)

Interview questions must be built. For senior positions, there is often a panel that will conduct interviews. Other ways, to work this process for lower-level grades is to have a supervisor conduct interviews and possibly a second person. Sometimes, it is just one person doing the interview depending on the normal daily work, the number of resumes, and the number of people who are available to conduct interviews. Sometimes, it will be just the hiring manager if people are not available or if it is a critical billet that needs to be filled soon.

The same interview questions are used on all selected applicants who have progressed to this point of interviews. This is done to make it a fair and equitable hiring process. The federal government hiring process is probably the most fair hiring process around. The federal government has built in over the years' legal protections and procedural protections for all manner of job applicants.

The top selectees will have reference checks initiated, which can also take time to get replies from the references. Sometimes, a reference may be on travel for a week or two and we need to wait for that reply. It is important for applicants to put references that are responsive and easy to contact.

While the interview is the process that most applicants see, there is so much more involved in the hiring action than applicants ever see. After all the work we have shown that the hiring manager has to do before you get to the point of interviewing an applicant, there is still much more to do. After the hiring manager has selected an applicant, and often 2 to 3 backups, that information is sent to the Civilian Personnel Office specialist who will contact the applicant with a hiring offer. We often find that the applicant was already hired, does not want to move, or is hoping for a different job. Now you see why the hiring manager is frustrated and then must go to his second choice. This also increases the time lag for getting a hiring action completed. The CPO specialist are the ones who are making the formal offers to the applicants. Thus, when there are changes those have to be communicated back and forth between see CPO and the hiring manager.

The Civilian Personnel Office security specialist will also start the security clearance process or verification of current security clearance. Sometimes, when a government employee is applying for a job outside of his department or agency, the process of formal job offers and security clearance verifications can take longer.

STORY: During one of the times that I was changing jobs, I received an offer letter from the U.S. Army. I was employed at that time at the Department of Energy. Both organizations take security seriously. When sending sensitive data, such as a Social Security number or pay data the information must be encrypted in email. You may not send sensitive data unencrypted. There is only one problem with this story, the encryption is not the same at all agencies. When the Army sent the email with that offer letter and I tried to open the encrypted letter, but it was unreadable.

It took three days for me to finally get someone to send my sensitive information unencrypted, so I could read it. There are many challenges to the hiring process. Maybe more challenges when it is across department or agency lines. It is very much worth the effort and very educational to move from department to department because you learn new ways of doing your job in a different environment. It does build up your skills.

Managers are often eager to get positions filled because it has taken months to get this far in the process. If this vacancy was caused by the retirement of are well skilled employee, many others in the office have had to pick up the slack to keep the organization operational. Everybody has been doing extra work because of the other person being gone. And as you see with the hiring process taking 3 to 6 months everyone is eager to get a new employee onboard and working.

Should I Send an Introduction Letter to a Federal Hiring Manager?

Three reasons I say HECK NO!

I recently wrote an article titled: *"5 Thoughts on Acquiring a Federal Job for Transitioning Military"* and as I had friends reviewing it, I got the question "Should I send an introduction letter to a federal hiring manager?" I have worked 36 years in the government both active duty, and a follow on career in civil. I started as a Private, and ended as a GG-15, the highest manager grade in federal service. I have been both the job hunter and the hiring manager.

I have had many people over the years send me emails when I got promoted. Often they had either their resume or a friend's resume in that email with strong suggestion for me to review and hire when there is an opportunity. I am sure we all love people to tell you how to do your job, and most of us may not react well to that. Below are some of my thoughts on receiving these emails or conversation:

1. **Inferior package submitted:** My first thought from an applicant that contacts me, or sends me more information that was asked in the USAJOBS web hiring portal is that the applicant believes they have a weak package. They are contacting me to get more information in front of me as a hiring manager. This is flat out not fair to the other applicants. Remember, most hiring managers were job hunters in the past. We all feel our package could have/should have had better information to make yourself more competitive. Even if you know you are missing information and it is past the deadline, suck it up, and move on. Do better on the next application.

2. **Ethical standards:** You send me an email or chat at a unit gathering trying to give me more information to make your package better looking. My first thought was above, but my reaction is that this person thinks that I am morally corrupt! They think they can gain illegal influence? Most hiring managers and I worked hard to get to their position with strong ethical standards as civil service employees Managers are getting closer to retirement and have a family. Why would these people think I endanger my job, family and retirement for someone I probably do not even know? We got to our positions by doing right and being fair. Giving assistance to one applicant over the others is not fair. As I stated in my past articles, I often had 200 qualified resumes per position.

3. **Sting operation:** I become curious as to why this person is asking for an illegal and improper favor during job hunting. There is the possibility that person, who is asking me for a hiring favor, is also working as part of a sting operation with the Inspector General Office, or a criminal investigative body.

Federal Jobs Need Strong, Ethical and Skilled Applicants

So if you are seeking a federal job, it is best NOT to send a letter of introduction and perhaps give the hiring manager the impression that you have an incomplete application package or weak ethical standards. Instead, focus on perfecting your job package to create a favorable impression on an impartial hiring manager.

All of this is going through my head when the nice person at the party, or someone sends an email that says, "Should I send an introduction letter to a federal hiring manager?" My answer is also in my head and without a doubt, the answer is HECK NO!!!

5 Thoughts on Acquiring a Federal Job

Since I recently retired from the federal service, I have many people asking me about how to get a federal job. This is especially true since I worked at three different agencies/departments both in the US and overseas with a security clearance. Additionally, I have been both the hunter and the hiring manager so it compounds matter and encourages people to ask me frequently about how to be successful in their job hunts.

In turn, here are a few best practices and lessons learned I have acquired over the years. They may not be perfect, all-encompassing but they should shed some light on some of the realities.

1. Do not submit one application for a career

Getting a Federal Government job takes time. I used to tell people that if you have not submitted at least 100 applications, I wouldn't take you seriously since you hadn't put in the time and effort necessary to secure your preferred position. In civil service in order to get a promotion or higher graded job you have to apply for a new job. So, I have been through the hunt many times to go from a GS-12 to a GG-15. Many people are hired every day in the Federal government. In 2014 the Office of Personnel and Management stated that the Federal executive branch had 2,663,000 civilian employees. That is not counting the almost 1.5 million uniformed military personnel and 63,000 legislative and judiciary branch personnel. There are over 4 million hired for the federal government. Many of them are working to get hired in different positions, locations and promotions. There is a system for hiring and it is working for those on the inside!

2. There are 4 million jobs in the federal government.

Getting a clearance is not easy, nor should it be easy. There are restrictions, and need for proof of good conduct and loyalty to USA. This makes sense if you want to have a well-protected country. If you think there is a problem with how your clearance was adjudicated, you need be willing to prove them wrong. The system gives you many opportunities to refute the decision.

Having been a hiring manager I can tell you that location makes a difference. For Intelligence and Security professionals, when I was hiring a civilian at Fort Monmouth, NJ, my referral list was short. The reason was simple; there were not a lot of Intelligence and Security professionals in that state. *(Lesson Learned: You have to go where the jobs are located.)*

When I was hiring for Intelligence and Security professionals at Aberdeen Proving Ground, MD, I doubt I ever had a referral list of fewer than 200 personnel applying for the job positions. The referral list sent to the hiring managers is prescreened applicants who meet the minimal requirements. That is a lot of resumes for managers to read!

Issues that can block your hiring, is that the government will have a change in the budget, staffing or mission. A new focus in hiring to get authority to hire due to budget uncertainty is to hire term positions. These are limited time positions that expire. You have no civil service rights at the end of the term. The proper name of those positions or jobs as stated in the regulation is Term Appointment.

There are risks for employees with the Term Appointments, but good employees can use these to climb to higher grades/ranks. Again, it is much riskier because you will be unemployed at the end of the term. But, you do have the ability to prove your worth in the federal workplace, receive awards, and build a resume. With the budget uncertainty this may be a future way for new employees to get hired. The completion is normally less for term employees.

One of the advantages for the taxpayers and managers is that it is similar to a probation system that can get rid of bad apples. If people do well on the term position, they will have a much-improved resume to get a better job.

When I was a hiring manager at Aberdeen Proving Ground (APG) in Maryland I had a large selection of applicants. We had approximately 20,000 personnel on post at APG. But, one-hour drive away were many more Intelligence and Security professionals at Fort Meade, MD. I would often get over 200 qualified resumes from the Civilian Personnel Office per job vacancy. Sometimes, I would receive 110 resumes with clearance, language, and technology skills that exceeded the needs for the current job.

3. Do not over inflate your worth compared to your experience.

Often a college student is aiming too high, and over estimates the value of their recently hard won degree. Degrees are great, but a degree with experience is outstanding.

Questions to ask:

What grade level have you been applying for?

Did you price yourself out of the market?

Are there 50 applicants with a degree and experience AND a desire for a lower grade than you?

4. Know the departments that are expanding

The portal for getting hired starts at www.usajobs.gov. They show on their first page the hot jobs/spotlights. Not a surprise is IT Specialist (Systems Engineer), Chief Information Security Officer (CISO), The Federal Bureau of Prisons, and The United States Capitol Police are all in the current spotlight for jobs. (This is a good indicator of where to find a federal job.)

Currently the US Secret Service (USSS) is hiring with many vacancies in both the Special Agent and Uniformed Division areas. They have a great webpage on how to get hired and help screen out personnel with potential security clearance problems. Their program is called The Special Agent and Uniformed Division Pre-Employment Review (SUPER) Interview.

> *The Special Agent and Uniformed Division Pre-Employment Review (SUPER) Interview is designed to: (1) provide applicants with realistic information about the Special Agent or Uniformed Division Officer positions and allow applicants to self-select out of the hiring process; (2) obtain information which may negatively impact an applicant's ability to obtain a Top Secret security clearance; and (3) assess relevant knowledge, skills, and abilities (i.e., competencies) needed for successful performance upon entry into the Special Agent and Uniformed Division Officer positions. Upon successful completion of the interview, applicants will receive a conditional offer of employment. From <http://www.secretservice.gov/join/apply/interview/>*

Many people start Civil Service taking one of the less sexy jobs to get their foot into the door. It is much easier to get hired as a current status employee than an outsider. This makes sense some position cannot use complete beginners and are at a higher level of performance then a starter job. Other jobs can allow some training time, to include training about civil service. You might need to live in an expensive area and commute for the job, but you get your foot in the door.

Watch the news and pay attention to organizations that are expanding. The US Border Patrol is often used as a starter job. In the past, they have had large expansions in staff needs resulting in plenty of job opportunities. The key is looking for where the jobs are located, and trying for those jobs. Do not be the person that thinks the federal government is going to bring you a tailored made job just for you, or modify everything for a beginner. Remember, there are a lot of people applying for the jobs and willing to take it without modification.

5. Go where the job is located.

Do you care where you get hired at, which location? If so, you are not really a serious job hunter. The goal is to get a job. The person who is looking for a Department of Defense GG-15 manager job in WY is going to be unhappy. (They do not have many DoD senior manager jobs there.) The government does not make a job in your favorite location. The jobs are where the work is needed.

Lastly, it irks me to hear people tell me that they applied for ONE job in the Federal government and they are waiting for the answer. They are not job hunters. They should go try to win the lottery. It makes the same sense. Job-hunting is a job, and you must apply for many jobs at the same time. Many times I have had two job offers to pick from when I was job hunting at the next level. The reason is that I applied for many jobs. I have told people, if you did not apply for one hundred jobs, you have not started job hunting.

Sorry if this sounds hard, it is best to get truthful information.... even if it is not happy information. (Now, go apply for 3 jobs today while you are upset.) That has been great therapy for me in the past!

Intelligence Professionals – Join an Association

Volunteers and members may gain leadership experience and improve networking opportunities while working with the association's leadership

All professionals should join a professional development association. It shows dedication to your career and career development. While this is for the Intelligence professional, the concept pertains to most other job series. There are associations for every job series. Google is your friend!

Professionals should join associations to build professional development and have an outlet to ask questions you would not want to ask in the office or of your boss. Associations allow you to meet people at various levels of the profession and offer development opportunities that prepare you for greater responsibilities in your career.

Most associations are non-profit organizations, which are often run by few, or no paid employees. Volunteers and members may gain leadership experience and improve networking opportunities while working with the association's leadership. When selecting an association, be sure to review those opportunities, often keys to determining good and bad. Other activities can include:

1) Representing member interests to state and federal lawmakers

2) Discounts and insurance

3) Newsletter or magazine covering activities and professional development

4) Distribution of news related to the profession [Related: Educational Opportunities in the Intelligence Field]

There are many associations for intelligence and national security, each of which has different qualifications or focus areas for members. Some offer student memberships and others may require dues based on rank or pay scale.

National Military Intelligence Association (NMIA)

The website states, "NMIA is a national association of intelligence professionals. NMIA seeks to stimulate awareness of the need for effective military intelligence as a critical component of national security. The Association also fosters activities and programs designed to enhance the theoretical and practical foundations of the intelligence discipline." This association is comprised of members throughout the intelligence community supporting all branches of military service. NMIA publishes the *American Intelligence Journal* and a newsletter. The association is probably best known for their ZGram™, an electronic newsletter containing news, resources, products, symposia, employment, and business opportunities.

ASIS International (Formerly, the American Society of Industrial Security)

The ASIS webpage notes, "ASIS International is the leading organization for security professionals, with more than 38,000 members worldwide. Founded in 1955, ASIS is dedicated to increasing the effectiveness and productivity of security professionals by developing educational programs and materials that address broad security interests, such as the ASIS

Annual Seminar and Exhibits, as well as specific security topics. ASIS also advocates the role and value of the security management profession to business, the media, government entities, and the public." ASIS crosses both homeland security and commercial industrial security. They produce a magazine for security managers. They offer student, member, and retired membership categories. Members are advocating a change in the retired age of 67 because many military and civil service security management professionals retire before that age.

Military Intelligence Corps Association (MICA)

The website notes, "MICA is the professional association of the U.S. Army's military intelligence corps. MICA members represent the active duty, reserve component, and retired Army (military and civilian) as well as defense contractors and others who support the MI mission and are dedicated to ensuring that Army Intelligence remains 'Always Out Front!' MICA is an Army-focused professional association that publishes the *Vanguard Journal*, which offers articles spanning the locations of the U.S. Army. MICA provides support to the Military Intelligence Museum, scholarships and mentoring activities. Chapters are strategically located across the globe. Recently MICA started an email distribution listserver and is exploring social media options. MICA sponsors the premier award for Army military intelligence—the Knowlton Award. The award was established in 1995 and MICA provides financial resources, administrative control, and publicity.

Marine Corps Counterintelligence Association (MCCIA)

The website speaks to the history and eligibility stating, "MCCIA is an independent, non-profit organization established in 1987 by a few CI men with a vision. The primary purposes of the association are to foster fraternal relations among retired, active, and former members of Marine Corps Counterintelligence while providing useful services for members and their dependents and survivors. Membership is open to Marines currently serving or having formerly honorably served in the active or reserve components of the United States Marine Corps; who have been awarded a counterintelligence Military Occupational Specialty by competent authority in accordance with Marine Corps directives in effect at the time of their service, and have honorably served as a Counterintelligence Marine. MICCA was the first DoD intelligence association to use a two-way email listserver to unite virtual associations with globe spanning membership. It was great tool to forge the fraternal link to both current and retired counterintelligence personnel. During the Global war on Terror, they were famous for their support to deployed counterintelligence personnel.

Army Counterintelligence Discussion Group (ACIDG)

One of the founders of ACIDG, Rick Eaton, stated, "The Army Counterintelligence Discussion Group mailing list is open to all active, reserve, former, and retired Army Counterintelligence Special Agents who held the Counterintelligence MOS to include ...civilians who are graduates of the US Army CI Special Agent Course...The primary purpose of the list is to discuss CI trends, news, current events, and history and serve as a general professional forum for current, former, and retired Army CI Special Agents to hold virtual discussions in a professional forum."

This is a no-cost professional development forum that originated in 1998. It has been a collaborative area to help new and retiring counterintelligence agents. It is often used to solve problems or find the history of regulations.

Association of Former Intelligence Officers (AFIO)

The webpage states, "AFIO is more than a professional or fraternal organization. Its distinguishing mission is educational...to reach out to the public and explain what intelligence organizations do, and to build a nation-wide constituency for intelligence as a profession. In many ways, AFIO is the public face of the Intelligence Community."

Most AFIO members are from the CIA but they also have a diverse population from other intelligence community members.

Operations Security Professionals Society (OPS)

The website notes, "The Operations Security Professionals Society (OPS) is a Maryland-based 501(c)6 whose purpose is to advance the interests of the United States and its allies by furthering the application of OPSEC as a professional discipline. Additionally, they serve as a means of educating and informing the American people with regard to the role of Operations Security in maintaining a strong national defense." OPS has newsletters and participates in the annual National OPSEC Conference hosted by the interagency OPSEC support staff. OPS established the OPSEC Certified Professional (OCP©) program to recognize individuals who meet the highest standards of the OPSEC profession.

Naval Intelligence Professionals (NIP)

"The website states, "The goal of the Naval Intelligence Professionals (NIP) is to further the knowledge of the art of maritime intelligence, and to provide a vehicle whereby present and former Naval Intelligence Professionals may be kept informed of developments in the Naval Intelligence community and of the activities and whereabouts of past shipmates." NIP has an excellent email list with timely and focused news pertaining to global intelligence. Many strategic watch standing analysts subscribe and discuss NIPMail contents. They have a job bank which is useful for transitioning sailors.

Summary

These are just a few of the many intelligence and national security professional organizations. Each individual must chart a path to career improvement. There is a role for seasoned professionals, too, as association leaders and mentors.

Do you have a Life Plan – Every Business has a plan

No business would start without a plan. Some have scratched out that plan on a napkin and later transformed it to a professional business plan to be presented at a bank or venture capitalist. To get a loan, a bank has to determine that the owners know where they are headed and have a plan.

Do people need a plan in life?

Many people do not have a plan. Very successful people make a plan and live by it. Plans make businesses successful. Should not people be successful?

1) Do you know what is your plan in the next five years or 10 years?

2) What is your plan for three years from now?

3) How are you going to accomplish your plan?

4) What concrete action have you performed to move forward to make success in life?

5) Did you follow a plan to further success?

Many times, the military will ask soldiers what is their plan, in 5 or 10 years. Many job interviews ask this question. Knowing what you are doing to move towards your five-year goal is good. Knowing what are your roadblocks to success is good. If you know what are the bumps in the road you can navigate it. In a Life Plan, you can identify the problem and start figuring out the solution. You can start figuring out the question to ask. Additionally, you can determine the person to ask the question to help you overcome the roadblock.

Problems like roadblocks, are solvable if you dissect the problem and find the person who will have the solution. If there is a police officer at the roadblock, you can go forward and ask for a solution, and they will normally direct you to the detour. If there is a flooded bridge, they will direct you to a bridge that is usable. Just as finding a person/mentor to help you find a solution to your problem, and maybe give you a different route, which you can safely follow to your destination of success.

To have a plan waiting for the future will not help. Waiting for an opportunity is like waiting for a winning lottery ticket. It is a plan, but doubtful of your ability to win, and have success.

Maps

If you are in New York City and want to drive to Los Angeles, would you hop into a car and start driving with no plan, no map or route? If you drive south, you may find it takes a long time to get to Los Angeles. Driving west is better. Having a map with the route on it is much better than guessing where you are going. Some people do more planning for a vacation trip than for having a successful life.

It is better able to focus on with what you are doing to fulfill your plan for your success. What are you doing to build your own plan? What are you doing to be able to retire successfully? There is time to make a plan and that is as early as possible in life. The plan may vary and go in multiple directions, and even the goals may be modified, but knowing where you are going is good.

It would be wonderful if schools would require a life plan to be created before the graduation. This would be good for both High School graduation and College Graduation. The responsibility is not on the school; the responsibility belongs to the "Life Owner" who must make their map for their journey.

Jumping in a car, without a map or a route is not a good idea. Just as not having a plan for life is not a good idea. Start making your plan for success today. Planning today, is better than tomorrow; today gives you an extra day to accomplish it!

Improving Your Marketable Job Skills

For most of us, having a job is critical to our finances, independence, and peace of mind. It is even a rite of passage for young people to be able to make it on their own. Probably the first factor to consider would be your current employment status. Being employed makes it much easier to jump to a better job. If you are not employed, you have to think about why employers aren't hiring you. It could be due to your lack of marketable job skills.

Conduct an Honest Assessment of Your Job Skills

Do you have the skills to be hired in the job you desire? Do you have the skills to acquire a higher-level job? Be sure your expectations are realistic. Some people will want a great job paying $150,000 a year, while they live in a city with a population of 700. However, those high-paying, high-skilled and high-responsibility jobs are in larger cities. To have a good career, be willing to move to new locations. Often, your new employer pays for that move.

How to Acquire Marketable Skills

If your marketable skills are low and not competitive in the marketplace, determine how to improve them. There are many possibilities.

Government Service

One way is to pick up new skills is through the military or the Peace Corps. The government has many ways where you can get skills while you earn a paycheck. For example, the military offers you an opportunity to get supervisory experience. These leadership roles could be adapted for a manager's job later on in the civilian world.

Business Internships

An internship is a great way to get your foot in the employer's door and prove your eagerness to learn job-related skills. Internships are also a way for the companies to scout for candidates to hire in the future. Many businesses have internship programs. Often, college staff will assist you in getting a summer intern job. At any time of year, you can also compete for internships online, so you do not have to depend on a school.

Volunteer Activities

Consider taking a volunteer job. In an April 2016 Forbes article, "How Volunteerism Can Help Kickstart Your Career," contributor Jules Schroeder stated, "Beyond being a personally gratifying and rewarding experience, volunteer work can do wonders for your resume. It's a testament to your character and helps you build a new skill set."

There are many online sites to search for volunteer jobs, such as VolunteerMatch or Idealist. Both have large job banks for both volunteers looking for jobs and employers posting jobs. Nonprofit organizations are a career field many people fail to explore. These organizations are good for short-term or long-term jobs and help you increase your experience. Nonprofits have both paid and unpaid jobs. Sometimes, it is worth taking an unpaid job to build your resume.

Continuing Education

College offers a way to improve your skill set and get skills desired in your career field. Although studying "Art of the 10th Century" may sound tempting, it may not give you the marketable skills you need for today's marketplace. Look for a school that offers courses that provide a solid contribution to your skill set. Consider online colleges, too. If you are pressed for time, online colleges provide you with more flexibility than traditional brick-and-mortar colleges. Accredited online colleges offer many bachelors and master's degrees.

If you are concerned about being able to afford college, there are many ways to get into college with financial assistance. Student loans and grants are plentiful; check with your school's financial aid office to learn about financial aid options. In addition, many employers such as the military, financial institutions and corporations offer tuition assistance. It is often surprising how many people do not take advantage of these educational opportunities.

For example, banks in large cities often offer tuition assistance to part-time employees who attend college. This way, banks get quality employees and improve employee retention. Similarly, corporations such as Walmart offer some paid positions at multiple levels where employees have access to professional training or college tuition assistance. Check on your current or potential employer's website to see if they offer these benefits.

Help is always welcomed – The Career Coach

There are many avenues to explore. There are Career Coaches in universities that are skilled in showing and guiding you to new solutions. Career Services conduct resume reviews and interview preparation in addition to giving needed updated advice.

More Marketable Skills May Lead to a More Satisfying Career

Building your marketable skills can improve your chances of being hired at a better job with a better paycheck. By taking advantage of volunteering opportunities, internships or other methods of improving your skills, you will be more prepared for the demands of the job market.

How to Take Advantage of Your Best Veteran Benefit?

June 22 is the 70th anniversary of the Servicemen's Readjustment Act of 1944, commonly known as the GI Bill. Since its inception, the GI Bill has impacted the United States socially, economically, and politically and has proven to be one of the greatest benefits offered to our veterans.

President Franklin D. Roosevelt signed the bill into law **on June 22, 1944. The** Veterans Administration is responsible for carrying out the law's key provisions: funding for education and training; loan guaranty for homes, farms or businesses; and unemployment pay. This allowed many veterans to enter the middle- class as educated professionals.

There were many problems during the demobilization following World War I, when discharged veterans received little more than a $60 allowance and a train ticket home. The GI Bill provided options that greatly assisted the assimilation of veterans into the workforce.

When the GI Bill was passed, some questioned the concept of sending WWII battle-hardened veterans to colleges and universities, a privilege then reserved for the rich. During the last 70 years, the program has brought positive change and improvements to veterans and to the country as a whole. It has allowed veterans the opportunity to attend schools that they would not have otherwise financially been able to attend. It allowed proven leaders to hone their skills in the civilian environment. It improved our education system by introducing the needs of a new type of student, leading to more diversity in the college experience.

Use it or lose it!

Over time, there have been many versions of the law, with most changes coming during or after different military events. I was a beneficiary of the Vietnam Era GI Bill.

Like many military careerists, I did not get a chance to use it while on active- duty. When I was retired, I was too worried about finding a job to think about school. As I settled down in the civilian workplace, I found my GI Bill benefit period slipping away. Veterans are allowed to use the GI Bill for 10 years after completion of military service, but forfeit the benefit if it is not used.

Unfortunately, many veterans let the benefit expire without taking advantage of the opportunities offered. I used my GI Bill towards the end of my 10- year time limit. In fact, my last class was not paid for by the GI Bill because my benefit expired. Getting a degree has opened many doors for me since that time. I am so glad I took advantage of the benefit and encourage all veterans to do so.

Getting started

Base/Post education centers can help any service member understand the benefits under the current GI Bill as well as education options. There are many programs that can help translate the skills learned in the military into civilian career skills. There are also many options for class format, from programs that invite veterans to live on a traditional campus, to programs that blend on- ground and online learning, to completely online programs.

Look for a school that has services to support veterans. For example, at American Military University where I teach, we offer fully-online classes that allow students to relocate, be deployed, and have other interruptions and still be able to continue a degree or certificate program. We also have faculty and academic and career counselors that are trained to support student veterans. Our online Virtual Veterans Center (VVC) serves as one central place where student veterans can access many services that are focused on their needs.

Finding the right college and program for you can take some research and effort, but the benefits afforded to you through the GI Bill are too valuable to pass up. Every veteran should be part of the GI Bill success story.

6 Military Traits That Transfer To Business Leadership

The military teaches decision-making just as college teaches elements of management

Many of the leadership traits learned in the military are as applicable in the business world as they are in one's personal life. While no single one could be considered the best, all contribute to a well-rounded person.

Military personnel can often do well in civilian business because service develops discipline. Those who do not think that the infantry teaches skills that are useable in the civilian business environment do not fully understand the lessons learned from being a squad leader or patrol leader. Military service cultivates initiative, an understanding of how to adapt to changes, the value of teamwork, and the discipline to accomplish the mission.

The Marine Corps offers a list of traits that characterize a good leader. All apply to the business environment as well. They include **1) judgment, 2) dependability, 3) integrity, 4) decisiveness, 5) courage, and 6) knowledge**.

Many people are a leader or NCO before leaving the military. While a young leader is in that position, they must also be tactful and unselfish. Enthusiasm, loyalty, and courage are often seen as military traits, but what business would not want enthusiasm and loyalty? Courage and integrity will help a business leader to unselfishly take the right action when needed.

The military teaches decision- making just as college teaches elements of management. The Marine Corps definition of exceptional decision-making would be valued by any business:

"Marines are prepared for anything because they train for a broad spectrum of situations. We develop Marines into leaders by constantly exposing them to training situations that require sound decisions with limited time, resources or information. Marines train to use their judgment, decisiveness and knowledge to respond quickly and appropriately because the worst decision a Marine can make in the midst of an operation is no decision at all."

In many parts of the business world, how you react to change or changing conditions can determine success. Just as a patrol leader must quickly respond to "contact on the right flank," a business has to respond to competitors bringing new products to the market. It is therefore valuable to have the traits and skills from the military, along with the adaptability to learn from business. It makes a winning combination.

Combining college education with the traits learned in the military further adds to the desired knowledge and skills. For employers, this combination offers them a college-educated person with discipline, skills, and a demonstrated ability to be a cohesive team player.

The Secrets of Federal Job Hunting Success

1. Secret number one is easy and makes the most sense. **THINK LIKE A HIRING MANAGER.** Review your resume and do not look at it as yourself or as an applicant. What would a manager see from that resume? Would they see anything that indicates a potential problem employee? Do you remind them of their wayward kid? Would they see an additional workload for themselves? Would they see an employee that would make their life easier?

2. **NEVER SUBMIT ONE APPLICATION** or wait for the results of that one application before submitting multiple other applications. If you have not submitted 100 applications, you have not started an employment search.

3. **FOR YOUR FIRST JOB APPLY FOR EVERYTHING AT THE LOWER LEVEL TO GET YOUR FOOT IN THE DOOR.** Apply for all available jobs in your qualifications, not your career path. This will allow you to get your first job in Federal government. Then, with experience and training it is easier to be more selective on future jobs.

4. **DEVELOP SKILLS NEEDED IN YOUR DESIRE CAREER FIELD.** This gives you a step ahead of other applicants. There is often training in multiple career areas in community colleges and universities. Every career field has an area you may be able to learn before you arrive. If you want to be an FBI, you will have to wait to go to the FBI Academy to learn some sensitive topics. All FBI agents have to

write reports. Every college teaches English and writings skills. You can develop skills before you enter desired career field.

5. **IN AN INTERVIEW DRESS FOR SUCCESS AND THE JOB YOU WANT.** People who go to an interview and believe that they should go comfortably, are people who are thinking of themselves. That is not what a hiring manager is looking for in a desirable applicant. People who take the time to wear suit and look professional shows they are motivated for the job. If you were the hiring manager, which person would you select, the person in blue jeans or the person in a suit? If you look like you barely have time to participate in the interview, or you are too busy to be bothered by this interview, you will remain unemployed. The person hiring you is looking for somebody who is motivated and who will help the organization to successfully meet the mission.

6. **WRITE AND GET PUBLISHED.** Create an image of being professional. Having good writing ability will make you more competitive than other applicants.

7. **SHOULD YOU DO INTERNSHIPS? WHEN?** Yesterday and heck yes! Internships teach arriving to work on time, doing as you are told, and being a team player. The more internships you have before you start your career, the more you will interest hiring managers. Internships provide training, and teach what is expected from you in a workplace environment. You may not learn great career skills, but you will learn the words HR, how to use the copier, how to do activities that you did not do in your short life in a school

environment. Grab internships in your high school summer vacations. Grab them in all of your college summer vacations. In fact, the federal government has some that you can do year round, to include your winter break. This helps build your resume.

Writing Can Improve Your Online Appearance

To Hiring Managers

Think of what would happen if a hiring manager were to look at your profile online. Would they see a fun loving wild young person? Would they first see the fun guy the bar who is very popular? Would the managers see multiple pictures in Facebook of a person with multiple partners?

This could be seen by the manager as a person that may be immature, undisciplined, a potential alcoholic, for a person who cannot commit. While you may see a fun loving wild person as the person you would want to go to the bar with, but would you want to be working with them in the next cubicle? Or would a counterintelligence or security screener view that as a put potential person who could not control their alcohol use since most pictures might be alcohol related? Would they see it as a commitment challenge person? If a guy is acting all the crazy on social media, did he think of how it would look to a future boss who is female?

Impressions are memorable and can kill an opportunity. You should review all your social media choices and think with someone else who does not know you would gleam from what they see. Don't make excuses, they will see the material without hearing your excuse. Often when you need excuses you are already in too far over your head.

Look for improvements in our social media and ensure that we are not embarrassed by the content. If your future boss was a former nun, you be embarrassed?

Writing articles will strengthen the view of your professional. It will strengthen others view of you. It will strengthen your understanding of your profession. Writing always helps define your communication keep building, structuring your thoughts, and thinking process.

There are many places where you write and get published. Where to get published depends on the type of article that the written. Some places can take months to approve an article, especially in peer review journals. Often your academic institution will have journals, E-Magazines, or even blogs. If you are working, your organization will probably have some type of workforce communication. Professional articles about whatever profession you are in will often have professional information outlets. Additionally, professional associations will have newsletters, websites, E-magazines, and blogs to share techniques, tactics, and procedures. Anytime you can write about how to make work faster or more efficient, this will help others believe you are a professional.

Most organizations are looking for content for their publications. Some larger organizations are overwhelmed by the amount of content they receive. Always research various publications and determine their timeline for publication and their rules.

Creating content that can get published about topics in the profession you desire to get hired will always improve your chances of getting hired. Having publications if your byline will show the hiring manager that you are a step above the rest of the pack of applicants desiring that position.

Opportunities for Bilingual Applicants

Authored by: Dr. Anna H. Lint

If you were born in another country with language ability (bilingual or multilingual) and naturalized US citizen, you are an extremely valuable asset for US government. US Citizens with a language are valuable for Intelligence organizations, FBI, DEA, DHS and obviously at the National Security Agency. The only exception, as indicated below, is for a non-US citizen linguist employed by Defense Language Institute Foreign Language Center (DLIFLC).

   ***According to DLIFLC website, "U.S. citizenship is not required for employment at DLIFLC, but proof of a work authorization must be submitted with the application. A limited number of H1B visas are sponsored by DLIFLC for qualified candidates in the necessary languages."

Story: I will use the alias "Jane" instead of her real name to protect her identity. Jane was born, raised, and educated in Korea, and went to graduate school in USA. She was a naturalized US citizen and wanted to work for US federal government to utilize her language ability. She applied for FBI and CIA. After the first application via each website of the organization, not a single organization contacted her. She worked for other private companies while she was pursuing those jobs. She was persistent and applied multiple times until she was contacted by them. FBI contacted her to take a language test, written test first and oral test later, and polygraphed her. Next, CIA contacted her to be interviewed and polygraphed. In some cases, if you are polygraphed, that polygraph accepted across the Intelligence Community and other government organizations. Reciprocity of polygraphs were part of an Executive Order, but there were a few exceptions to required reciprocity. There are now experts in organizations using the exception to the E.O. It is not infrequent to see another agency that will require an additional polygraph specifically for their standards. This is especially true with the diverse mission space of the FBI and CIA.

From above information, you would learn that you should be persistent to be hired by the organization you want. Even if you have been rejected multiple times, never give up. When the time is up for you, you will be selected. US needs your language skill and cultural awareness to build the constructive understanding of diversity of the world. Continue to look for the employers that value and utilize your linguistic capability and cultural knowledge in a certain area.

I provide some organizations that you can apply for, jobs that you may be interested in, and the quotes for job descriptions from each website below:

1. Federal Bureau of Investigation (FBI)
2. Central Intelligence Agency (CIA)
3. National Security Agency (NSA)
4. Defense Intelligence Agency (DIA)
5. U.S. Department of State
6. Defense Language Institute (DLI)/ Defense Language Institute Foreign Language Center (DLIFLC)
7. Department of Homeland Security (DHS)
8. Drug Enforcement Administration (DEA)

Federal Bureau of Investigation (FBI)

SPECIAL AGENTS: "The Special Agent Selection System is a mentally and physically challenging process designed to find only the most capable applicants. However, those who make it through the process become part of an elite team that keeps our country safe" (FBI website, https://www.fbijobs.gov/career-paths/special-agents).

INTELLIGENCE ANALYSTS: "Intelligence Analysts break down information into key components and contribute to plans of action to understand, mitigate and neutralize threats. This means they are part of our first line of defense for national security" (FBI website, https://www.fbijobs.gov/career-paths/intelligence-analysts).

LANGUAGE ANALYSTS: "FBI Linguists use their knowledge of other cultures and languages to help the FBI fulfill its mission to protect the United States from threats both international and domestic. Linguists work with a team to defend the country against foreign counterintelligence threats, cases of corruption, espionage, cybercrime and other unlawful offenses. All FBI Linguists begin their careers as Contract Linguists" (FBI website, https://www.fbijobs.gov/career-paths/language-analysts).

Central Intelligence Agency (CIA)

ANALYTIC POSITIONS: "CIA analysts are skilled subject-matter experts who study and evaluate information from all available sources—classified and unclassified—and then analyze it to provide timely and objective assessments" (CIA website, https://www.cia.gov/careers/opportunities/analytical).

BUSINESS, IT & SECURITY POSITIONS: "The range and variety of Business, IT and Security occupations is extensive, with high-level qualifications for every position. Generally speaking, we look for individuals who see their career as more than a job and will take on our mission in a personal way, applying their skills and talents for the good of the country" (CIA website, https://www.cia.gov/careers/opportunities/support-professional).

DIRECTORATE OF OPERATIONS (FORMERLY KNOWN AS THE CLANDESTINE SERVICE): "The DO seeks candidates with a variety of backgrounds, life experience, and professional and educational histories. Candidates must have (or be within one year of earning) a 4-year degree from an accredited college or university" (CIA website, https://www.cia.gov/careers/opportunities/clandestine).

LANGUAGE POSITIONS: "The ability to speak, translate, and interpret foreign languages, in addition to understanding cultural differences, is vital to the mission of the Central Intelligence Agency" (CIA website, https://www.cia.gov/careers/opportunities/foreign-languages).

National Security Agency (NSA)

INTELLIGENCE ANALYST: "Collect, analyze and report intelligence that uncovers the intentions of foreign governments and non-state entities worldwide" (NSA website, https://www.intelligencecareers.gov/nsa/nsacareers.html).

LANGUAGE ANALYST: "Uses knowledge of foreign language and English to provide key decision makers with a complete and accurate picture of the context within which the decision is being made" (NSA website, https://www.intelligencecareers.gov/nsa/nsacareers.html).

FOREIGN LANGUAGE ADVISOR: "Serve in a position where your contributions can have a positive effect on a global scale. The Intelligence Community has many opportunities for foreign language analysts" (NSA website, https://www.intelligencecareers.gov/nsa/nsacareers.html).

Defense Intelligence Agency (DIA)

FOREIGN LANGUAGES: "In general, DIA does not employ individuals due to foreign language skills alone. There are only a very small number of translator or interpreter positions. Foreign language proficiency is considered in hiring decisions for intelligence officers. As an incentive, you can supplement your salary if you qualify for Foreign Language Proficiency Pay (FLPP)." (DIA website, http://www.dia.mil/Careers/Foreign-Languages).

U.S. Department of State

CONSULAR FELLOWS PROGRAM: "The Consular Fellows Program offers candidates a unique opportunity to serve their country, utilize their foreign language skills, and develop valuable skills and experience that will serve them well in follow-on professions" (State dept. Website, https://careers.state.gov/work/foreign-service/consular-fellows).

FOREIGN SERVICE OFFICER: "If you're passionate about public service and want to represent the U.S. around the world, a challenging and rewarding career is waiting for you. The opportunity to work and experience cultures, customs and people of different nations is truly a career unlike any other" (State dept. Website, https://careers.state.gov/work/foreign-service/officer).

FOREIGN SERVICE SPECIALIST: "The U.S. Department of State offers career opportunities to professionals in specialized functions needed to meet Foreign Service responsibilities around the world" (State dept. Website, https://careers.state.gov/work/foreign-service/specialist).

Defense Language Institute (DLI)/ Defense Language Institute Foreign Language Center (DLIFLC)

EMPLOYMENT: "Positions are open to all U.S. citizens and other individuals eligible for or holding valid / current U.S. work authorizations. U.S. citizenship is not required for employment at DLIFLC. However, proof of work authorization must be submitted with the application. A limited number of H1B visas are sponsored by DLIFLC for qualified candidates in the necessary languages" (DLIFLC website, http://www.dliflc.edu/administration/employment).

REQUIRED QUALIFICATIONS: A four year accredited university degree is the minimum requirement.

LANGUAGE EVALUATION: The minimum required English proficiency is a LEVEL 2 and the minimum proficiency for the language to be taught is a LEVEL 3 in speaking as defined by the Interagency Language Roundtable (ILR) Skill-Level descriptions, found at the government ILR website. All language tests are performed telephonically.

FOREIGN DEGREES: If you have a degree from a non-U.S. educational institution it will need to be evaluated in order for your application to be considered.

Department of Homeland Security (DHS)

LAW ENFORCEMENT CAREERS: "Law enforcement careers involve protecting the President, Vice President, their families, heads of state and other designated individuals. These careers also involve securing the nation's borders, interagency law enforcement training, and enforcing economic, transportation and infrastructure security" (DHS website).

- U.S. Customs and Border Protection

- U.S. Immigration and Customs Enforcement

- U.S. Secret Service

- Federal Protective Service

- Federal Law Enforcement Training Center

IMMIGRATION AND TRAVEL SECURITY CAREERS: "Immigration and travel security careers involve protecting the nation's transportation systems, as well as overseeing lawful immigration to the U.S." (DHS website).

- Transportation Security Administration

- U.S. Citizenship and Immigration Services

PREVENTION AND RESPONSE CAREERS: "Prevention and response careers protect the public, environment and U.S. economic and security interests. These careers also provide preparedness, protection, response, recovery and mitigation to reduce loss of life and property and protect the nation from all hazards" (DHS website).

MISSION SUPPORT CAREERS: "Mission support careers involve the following fields: medical, human resources, facilities, budget, procurement, science and technology, training, intelligence, public affairs, communication, planning and coordination, detection, civil rights, fraud detection and more" (DHS website).

Drug Enforcement Administration (DEA)

EMPLOYMENT REQUIREMENTS: "All applicants must meet the certain conditions of employment to be eligible for employment at DEA" (DEA website).

1) U.S. Citizenship

2) Successfully passing a DEA-administered drug test for illegal drugs

3) Completion of a DEA Drug Questionnaire and Drug Use Statement to show compliance with the DEA Drug Policy

4) Successfully passing a background investigation

5) Registration with the Selective Service System, if male and born after 12/31/1959

Why Culture Knowledge Matters For National Security

The U.S. military has found that linguists are helpful in both routine and high-stakes events

By Dr. Anna H. Lint and James R. Lint (Originally Published at:
https://www.military1.com/international/article/458208-why-culture-knowledge-matters-for-national-security)

Throughout our history, many people in America have learned English as a second language. French, German, and Spanish immigrants were followed by Italians and other Europeans. Later came an influx of Asians. Most immigrants have integrated and learned English for their own needs, but these non-native English speakers have also benefited national security.

The U.S. military has used linguists to help with their knowledge of both languages and cultures. This can be helpful in routine situations like coordinating port visits of American flagged ships. It can also be helpful in higher stakes events, like trying to bring about a cease-fire between two combating forces.

Roots in Korean War

Personnel who serve as mediators need to know more than the language — they need to be culturally attuned to prevent inadvertent embarrassments by offending one of the parties. The military has used different programs for helping overcome language divides. One of the most well known is in Korea, where the language is difficult to learn. The Korean Augmentees to the U.S. Army (KATUSA) program was started during the Korean War with native laborers who carried ammunition and helped rebuild areas under U.S. guidance. This program has since generated some of the best English linguists in Korea, including college students who compete to participate.

There are many requirements for the knowledge of non-English languages and cultural understanding in the intelligence world. People who learned English as a second language often have a better understanding of culture and cultural differences that can impact human relations.

Resources for learning a language

While non-native English speakers may have a natural edge, the right training can prepare anyone to work effectively across languages and cultures. The U.S. Army, National Security Agency, and State Department all have good schools for linguistics that integrate culture into the classes. Some examples are the **Defense Language Institute**, the U.S. Department of State **Foreign Service Institute**, the National Security Agency **STARTALK Language Program**, and the **U.S. Army Language Program**.

Non-government personnel can get language training in the U.S. and in other countries. One leading worldwide language training company is **Berlitz**. Germany offers the inexpensive **Volkshochschule** program, while South Korea's famous **Yonsei University** teaches Korean language and culture.

Many colleges and community colleges also have language training programs and electives or programs that focus on a foreign language and culture. An inexpensive method for learning may be to volunteer as an ESL instructor at a local school. Business travel, church trips, or a tour with the **Peace Corps** can also provide opportunities to learn language and culture.

No doubt, any opportunity to learn about additional languages and cultures will benefit any career in national security and beyond. We live in a global world, and many careers in the future will likely require the ability to work effectively beyond U.S. borders.

The Lessons of International Travel Can Help with Career Success

One of the advantages of international travel is that we get a chance to see and explore new areas. In the military we must travel; in corporate business, we must travel when told. The positive side of this is that you get to see new or different ways to do something.

This learning is good because your experiences build you into a more successful employee. Your employer will be surprised at the ideas you come up with that are unique in the part of the world he lives in, but normal in another part of the world. This is the value of foreign travel.

The problem is that we often do not assess the new ideas until we have free time. With family, jobs, and school pursuits, we often do not look around and realize what we have experiences that we can learn from. An excellent case in point is a trip I took to Korea after I retired. I was not working and it was a relaxing trip. Afterwards, I had time to reflect on what I experienced and I realized I had learned many valuable things during the trip. Reflection often creates learning.

An example of learning with the potential to reuse the idea in another part of the world would be a unique technique the Korean Airlines uses for customer service on long flights or when customers may be sleeping during the time of the delivery of services or food. How does the steward staff know to wake a person or let him or her sleep?

Korean Airlines has a simple and cost effective answer. They have a paper about five inches by seven inches that has three colored stickers that have a picture on the top that is simple to understand without translation. Then they have in bold the information in the international language of English. Next, in smaller type, is Korean, Japanese, and Chinese.

The stickers say, "Please do not disturb; please wake me for duty free (with gift box picture); and please wake me for meal service." In all four languages is a note at the bottom that says "Please place the sign on to your headrest for your convenience." Most people put them on the seat in front of their seat, just above the fold down table.

It was a great idea, although I can see better English instructions as a potential improvement. Keeping customers fed, buying duty free goods, or sleeping is an example of enhancing customer service. Not waking up and making an upset customer who would not desire to do duty free shopping is effective customer service. On the other hand, if the correct customers are alerted for the duty free shopping, they will add to Korean Airline's bottom line.

Success in business means bringing new ideas to the table. Military experience and foreign travel teach us more ways to accomplish the mission. College teaches us ways to learn, analyze, and reflect to create unique learning points based on our experience and training. These are the tools that educated employees can bring to the employer to enhance their success.

Edward Snowden and the Legal Methods of Reporting Complaints

The White House's petition system "We the People" has a request to pardon NSA contractor and whistleblower Edward Snowden. Started in 2013, the request received 167,955 signatures from people who want Snowden to receive a full pardon for his actions.

In more recent actions, the American Civil Liberties Union (ACLU) is calling for clemency to be shown to Snowden. The ACLU launched a new website, www.pardonsnowden.org, to motivate site users to urge President Obama to give Snowden a presidential pardon. Should Snowden be pardoned or should the opposite occur – a charge of treason?

Was it Treason?

Edward Snowden gave both China and Russia classified information regarding Prism, a U.S. government warrantless surveillance program. The program enabled the NSA to monitor American citizens.

In a 2013 interview with U.K. news source The Guardian, Snowden explained his reasons for disclosing the NSA's secret eavesdropping on Americans' phone conversations. He wanted to "inform the public as to that which is done in their name and that which is done against them."

Snowden hoped that people would use his information to debate the issue of privacy. Most people claim that what Snowden did is wrong or even treasonous, but Snowden sees his actions very differently.

The White House has made its position clear. According to a September 2016 article in the Washington Post, the White House says that Snowden should return to the U.S. to face charges for leaking classified information.

'Snowden' Movie Debut May Create Atmosphere for Presidential Pardon

Oliver Stone's movie, "Snowden," comes out this week with Joseph Gordon-Levitt in the starring role. The movie increases the pressure for the president to pardon Snowden at the end of his term.

Many presidents give controversial pardons at the end of their presidential terms. The conditions, including the release of the movie, may well hasten a presidential pardon in the coming weeks.

Snowden Could Have Sought Other, More Legal Methods for Privacy Complaint

When Snowden worked at the NSA, he seemed to disagree with the current laws and had a different interpretation of his former employer's compliance with the law. Apparently, Snowden did not know the correct way to have a disagreement and the legal way to correct the NSA's actions.

Snowden's inexperience with the NSA may have impacted his decision. Snowden only worked at NSA Hawaii for three months.

Snowden Bypassed Government's Formal Complaint Process

In the Department of Defense (DoD), there is a formal path to report sensitive or classified problems. The DoD Hotline provides a confidential avenue for individuals to report allegations of wrongdoing pertaining to programs, personnel and operations that fall under the purview of the Department of Defense, pursuant to the Inspector General Act of 1978.

Anyone may file a complaint with the DoD Hotline. That includes members of the public and DoD employees (military members, civilian employees and DoD contractors).

There are three types of complaints:

- Fraud, waste or abuse: Report fraud, waste, abuse and mismanagement regarding programs and personnel under the purview of the U.S. Department of Defense.

- Whistleblower reprisal: Report adverse personnel actions taken against an individual because that individual made or was thought to have made a protected communication.

- Classified information: Report wrongdoing involving classified information.

There are separate, defined processes for submitting complaints that involve secret and top-secret information. However, it appears that Snowden chose not to use the DoD's traditional complaint process.

Federal Whistleblower Act Would Have Offered Protection for Snowden

The Intelligence Community Whistleblower Protection Act (ICWPA) of 1998 provides a secure means for employees to report classified problems to Congress. ICWPA spells out a process by which employees of the Defense Intelligence Agency, National Geospatial-Intelligence Agency, National Reconnaissance Office, and the National Security Agency can report matters of urgent concern to the intelligence committees of Congress.

Despite its name, this act does not grant special statutory protection for whistleblowing intelligence community employees from reprisal, because they already are protected according to other laws. All federal employees are protected against reprisal for engaging in certain protected activities via other applicable federal antidiscrimination or whistleblower protection laws.

Correct Reporting of Complaints Helps National Security

Without a doubt, fixing problems regarding federal fraud, waste and abuse is important. Reporting violations of wrongdoing involving classified information is critical to the protection of sensitive operations.

However, it is important to understand the correct options for reporting complaints. There are better ways to complain that will not adversely impact national security, your career or your life.

The DoD Hotline at 1-800-424-9098 (an unsecured line) is a great place to start. The staff there can handle questions or concerns and will point you toward the proper channels if they can't handle your complaint themselves. In addition, federal special security offices and intelligence and security offices are prepared to help individuals determine the proper complaint process.

Snowden's Current Situation Serves as Reminder to Complain Legally

People who work in national security have a responsibility to the country to make complaints using the proper tools and processes. The system works, and many employees have utilized the process.

Unfortunately, for Snowden, he had only worked at his job for three months. He did not know the full process for data collection or the safeguards in place.

For much of his time at the NSA, Snowden did not have security authorization, therefore he did not understand the Prism program. He might have found that safeguards were in place and he apparently did not have all of the information to determine if there truly was a violation.

There are classified measures in place to successfully make complaints to the federal government. If Snowden had pursued legal channels to make his point about privacy, his life may have been significantly different than it is now.

Epilogue

In closing, the ideas shared in this book work. It worked for me in a 38-year career in the military, contracting, and Federal Civil Service. This career took me from being an infantry Private in the US Marine Corps to an Army GG-0132-15, Director of Intelligence and Security for an Army 2 star General Officer level command.

I had 25 moves from Marine Corps boot camp to my final retirement move. Part of my success was a willingness to relocate. (In Civil Service, it is mostly optional.) FBI, MICECP, and a few other programs require relocations every 3-5 years. Moves are good, you learn in different offices, jobs, and parts of the world. Dr. Anna, my wife, has always obtained a higher level job after moving. It can be done. She did it with increasing education and jobs with increased responsibility.

I have traveled all over the Mediterranean as a US Marine on a Navy ship; I went to Korea for a year pre and during the 1988 Olympics working sensitive support; to Fort Meade, MD; and then to Germany; to Georgia; to Gitmo for the Cuban Boatlift 1994-95; to Georgia; to Korea; to Fort Meade, MD; to Washington DC; to Korea for almost 5 years in civil service; to Washington DC DHS HQ; to Department of Energy, Germantown, MD; to New Jersey, and to Aberdeen Proving Ground, Maryland, where I later retired and made my final move. There are many opportunities in that long run on sentence! There were many other moves in the early Marine Corps life. Each move was a learning event and built on my ability to obtain future jobs with more responsibility and pay.

Another SECRET was that we often lived very close to the job. In Korea, I was often a mile away from my office. At DHS in Washington DC, I lived two buildings in an apartment from my office. In Germantown, MD at

Department of Energy, we lived about a two-minute drive, unless the traffic light was red. Being close to, the office was an advantage when many of my co-workers were commuting 60-90 minutes in Washington DC traffic.

I competed for jobs in Korea, (won), Japan, (declined due to better job offer at the same time,) and winning multiple jobs in Washington, DC, Maryland, and New Jersey. Competing for jobs also taught me about different departments in the US Government. Doing job interviews all over Washington, DC, showed me areas of the government that could help either in my current or future job.

The multiple organizations both military and DHS and DOE made me much more competitive than my co-workers who were only employed in a single agency. To manage your career, you have to step out of your comfort zone and gain new talents by observing that there is more than one process to accomplish the mission. This allows you to be more competitive and gain higher pay grades.

The best part of this journey and the biggest secret is that I had fun! I hope you will also have a great Federal Government career.

I have created a public general advertising Facebook page at https://www.facebook.com/SecretsToGettingaFederalGovernmentJob/ . To get into the private Facebook page please connect to me in a private message at Facebook or LinkedIN. If you have a specific question that is the area for those questions that I offer as a service to those readers of this book.

I will create a second Facebook site that will allow you to ask questions about the hiring process and getting a federal civil service job. (I will continue the discussion started in this book about, "Should I Send an Introduction Letter to a Federal Hiring Manager? -- Three reasons I say

HECK NO." This could keep you out of jail and out of the eye of upset hiring managers. I have created one public site and one private group and those people who have bought the book will have a way to enter that group through the answer of a question about the book. (The question MAY be what is the 5th letter in the 3rd chapter, or a similar question.) You will have a resource to get any questions not answered in this book, successfully answered for your career search. I hope to invite a friend who is a Civilian Personnel Office administrator. She is currently in the system and deals with every day hiring problems.

There is NO promise of a job just because you buy this book. You must research job announcements for your job. We will give you some details and methods; you have to create a good resume for the job you desire. Your competition is going to be good. You have to evaluate your skills against the job vacancy.

All profits and proceeds from the book will go to the Lint Center for National Security Studies where we give scholarships for people looking to grow in the national security field. See www.LintCenter.org for scholarship and volunteering opportunities.

James R Lint

https://www.facebook.com/jim.lint.5

https://www.linkedin.com/in/jimlint/

Biographies of Authors

James R. Lint, Author

SUMMARY:

Retired on 30 August 2014 from federal Civil Service as Director, Intelligence and Security, G2, US Army Communications Electronics Command, GG-0 132-15. Retired military, 7 years US Marine Corps, 14 years US Army. Retired Counterintelligence Special Agent. Awarded Intelligence Community Joint Duty Assignment Credit. Non-Profit Charity Management from 2007. National Vice President of Military Intelligence Association (MICA) 2014. Currently, 2017, *Senior Editor for* In Cyber Defense *& Contributor,* In Homeland Security.

Mr. James R. Lint retired on 30 August 2014 from federal Civil Service as Director, Intelligence and Security, G2, US Army Communications Electronics Command, GG-0132-15. Since 2010, Professor at American Military University teaching management. In November 2014, elected to be the National Vice President of the Military Intelligence Corps Association (MICA). He served in the United States military for over 20 years, in both the U.S. Marine Corps (7 years) and U.S. Army (14 years). He spent four years as a Marine Counterintelligence specialist and nearly 15 years as an Army Counterintelligence Special Agent. Lint has expertise in counterintelligence, cyber security and information assurance, terrorism and counterterrorism, human intelligence collection and prevention, as well as low-intensity asymmetric warfare.

Mr. Lint was appointed as the US Army CECOM Director, Intelligence and Security (G2) in Feb 2008 and retired in 2014. As the Director of the G2, he has direct responsibility for management of the G2 Office. The mission of the G2 Office is to provide command-wide staff support for the functional areas of Security Management, Intelligence Threat, Special Security, and Technology Protection. Mr. Lint has served as the Deputy Director for Safeguards & Security, Office of Science, for the U.S. Department of Energy (DOE). While at the DOE, Mr. Lint ushered through Congress two budgets and oversaw 10 national laboratories security operations with an annual Safeguards and Security budget of $81 million. Previously, Mr. Lint served at Department of Homeland Security (DHS), Office of Intelligence and Analysis where he was initially the lead cyber intelligence analyst and later the Chief of the Collection Analysis Team.

Mr. Lint attained the rating of Senior Instructor at the U.S. Army's Intelligence Center and School, Fort Huachuca, AZ where he trained enlisted personnel, allied officers, and U.S. officers in the art of military intelligence and counterintelligence. During his tenure, he won the Department of Human Intelligence Instructor of the Month competition for his contributions. Throughout his military career, Lint spent considerable time in overseas theaters including postings to Cuba, Europe

& the Mediterranean, as well as numerous tours in Korea. Additionally, he spent several years as a government contractor, supporting the Army's Intelligence and Security Command for Systems Test and Evaluation at Fort Belvoir, Va. Shortly thereafter, as part of a Civil Service assignment, he spent nearly 5 years as the Deputy Director for Intelligence & Security with the 1st Signal Brigade in Yongsan, Seoul, Korea.

Mr. James Lint's personal decorations and commendations include: the DOE Superior Performance Award, the DHS Performance Award, the Joint Meritorious Achievement Award, the Humanitarian Service Medal, the Korea Defense Medal and 5 Meritorious Service Medal's.

Mr. Lint has an M.B.A. with a concentration in Information Technology Management, from Touro University International. Additionally, he is a graduate of the near year-long OPM Management Development Center's Senior Leadership Cohort Program at Aberdeen Proving Ground, MD.

Mr. Lint has written extensively on counterintelligence, military intelligence, and Korea. He has also been selected as an advisor on the APUS Graduate and Undergraduate Intelligence Studies Industry Advisory Council.

FEB 2016: Became an Associate Member of the Military Writers Guild

The Military Writers Guild exists to gather writers committed to the development of the profession of arms through the exchange of ideas in the written medium. Learn more at http://militarywritersguild.org/.

Past Publications Authored

First book titled, "Leadership and Management Lessons Learned, A Book of Management Vignettes." - The Kindle Edition went on sale at Amazon.com on October 17, 2013. This book was about the difference leadership and management styles in the federal government and is a great companion book to the "Secrets of Getting a US Federal Government Job". All profits and proceeds go to the Lint Center for National Security Studies scholarship program. We encourage you to look and help spread the word. The book is available for purchase here: http://www.amazon.com/dp/B00G04EG1E . - See more at: http://lintcenter.info/blog/entry/3703514/must-read-leadership-and-management-lessonslearned#sthash.KnjZsbti.dpuf

Second book Co-Authored with Dr. Anna Lint, "8 Eyes on Korea, A Travel Perspective of Seoul, Korea." Multiple perspectives of Korea from both Americans and Koreans. FEB 2016 Release. http://www.amazon.com/dp/B01BAEVN7I All proceeds go to charity. Great contributors!

Articles:

Sequester and Furloughs: It's Discount Espionage Time, July 15, 2013 Published by Homeland Security Today, By: James Lint and Timothy W. Coleman. Same article also reprinted in OPSEC Professional Society Newsletter and Military Intelligence Professional Bulletin Memories of a day in June. Published by Monmouth Messenger June 26, 2009. A Story about Security and Intelligence Failure in June 1950 and thoughts of Security and Intelligence professionals today. By 1950, the U.S. Army had just finished World War II five years earlier. The Army had a major drawdown and had cut troop units and staff. Most of the junior personnel had not even served in World War II. No draftees had combat experience. June 25, 1950 was a nice summer day with people preparing for a post softball event. The weather was wonderful. It was a great day to forget the office and to enjoy life, even if you were stationed in Korea. That day was a day for Operations Security (OPSEC) and a busy day for many—especially for North Koreans emptying their motor pools and moving troops south to attack South Korea.

Mr. Lint has written extensively on counterintelligence, military intelligence, and Korea.

Amazon Author Page: http://www.amazon.com/James-Lint/e/B00G1749LC/

Dr. Anna Hyonjoo Lint, Author

Summary:

Dr. Anna Hyonjoo Lint, Ph.D. in Educational Leadership, has spent more than 30 years in both the public and private sector, including senior level positions in the financial services sector, as well as in academia, in both the United States and South Korea. Currently Dr. Lint teaches graduate level students at Trident University.

Previous:

*Dr. Anna H. Lint started as a successful small business entrepreneur, securing a handsome profit on a brick and mortar bookstore venture that she built from the ground up.

*Professor in the English Language Department at the Jangan College and Samsung Corporate Instruction Center in South Korea.

*As Managing Director of a major land development company, she oversaw and directed more than 500 residential units in both Seoul and Incheon. While working in the private sector, she was also responsible for managing more than 200 foreign language instructors at The ACE Global Education Center for Foreign Languages, as part of a corporate feeder partnership and strategic management program, for Samsung Co., LG, Hyundai Motor Co. of Korea, and Daewoo Motors.

*Dr. Anna H. Lint worked as Bank Officer for Chevy Chase Bank, CitiBank, Nara Bank, and Bank of America.

Volunteerism and Service:

Dr. Anna H. Lint is a co-founder of Lint Center for National Security studies. Dr. Lint, as a constant community volunteer, has dedicated her time and expertise to the Army Family Support Group of 1st Signal Brigade in Yongsan, Korea. In addition, she taught English to those in need at the Vietnamese Refugee Center in Oklahoma City, Oklahoma.

Education:

PhD, Educational Leadership, Trident University, concentrated in E-Learning,

MA, TESOL (Teaching English to Speakers of Other Languages) from Oklahoma City University.

MA, Industrial Design, with a concentration in Interior Design from Ewha Womans University, Seoul, Korea

BS, Home Economics, Dongduk Women's University, Seoul, Korea

Written Works:

Lint, A. & Lint, J. (2016). 8 Eyes on Korea, A Travel Book. Amazon Digital Services LLC. http://www.amazon.com/dp/B01BAEVN7I

Lint, A. & Lint, J. (2014, January). Why culture knowledge matters for national security. *Military1.*
http://www.military1.com/international/article/458208-why-culture-knowledge-matters-for-national-security

Lint, A. (2013, Winter). Academic Persistence of Online Students in Higher Education Impacted by Student Progress Factors and Social Media. *Online Journal of Distance Learning Administration, 16*(4).
http://www.westga.edu/~distance/ojdla/winter164/lint164.html

Lint, A. (2013). E-learning Student Perceptions on Scholarly Persistence in the 21st Century with Social Media in Higher Education. *Creative Education, 4*(11). http://www.scirp.org/journal/ce/

Lint, A. (2011). The Impact of Student Progress Factors on Student Persistence in E-learning.
Power Point Presentation, Lint Center for National Security Study, Inc. website:
http://www.lintcenter.org/Leadership/Alint.htm

Past Books and Charities of Authors

All funds from book sales go to the below charity.

Charity

Mission Statement:

The mission of the Lint Center for National Security Studies is to foster and further the educational development and opportunities for the next generation of America's Counterintelligence and National Security Workers. The Center focuses on empowering individuals, enhancing the study of national security issues, and enabling emerging leaders to be mentored by established current-and-former industry experts.

Description:

The Lint Center for National Security Studies, Inc., founded in 2007, is a non-profit 501 (c) (3) organization created to award merit-based scholarships for Counterintelligence and National Security Workers, their children and scholars, and to advance the study of National Security, cross-cultural studies, and global understanding.

The Center aims to:

1. Identify promising individuals and assist in educational pursuits through scholarship initiatives

2. Provide talented individuals with a meaningful leadership development mentoring program by current-and-former Counterintelligence and National Security Workers

3. Create a forum for the dissemination and discussion of National Security Studies through the Center's online Web-portal

- All donations and contributions to the Lint Center are allocated solely to the Center's scholarship funds.
- All actions and activities by the Lint Center are conducted by unpaid staff and volunteers.
- The Center is Veteran and minority operated and managed.

The Lint Center for National Security Studies, Inc., was founded in 2007, as a non-profit 501(c)(3) charitable organization that was created to award merit-based scholarships and to provide mentoring programs for individuals pursuing careers in intelligence, counterintelligence and national security.

More than 200 mentors, seasoned practitioners in their field, volunteer through the Lint Center to show younger people what they can do in the Intelligence Community. This enhances the study of national security issues, cross-cultural studies, global understanding, cyber intelligence, and creates a natural bridge for the next generation to acquire knowledge about the industry, as they consider career options.

Established current-and-former industry experts mentor emerging leaders to provide invaluable insight to those who wish to follow in the footsteps of national service. Scholarships are awarded biannually in July and January.

Past Books

https://www.amazon.com/Leadership-Management-Lessons-Learned-Vignettes-ebook/dp/B00G04EG1E/	**Leadership and Management Lessons Learned, A Book of Management Vignettes.** Book covers Management in Military, Civil Service, and Corporate World for almost 40 years by James Lint (Author)
https://www.amazon.com/Eyes-Korea-Travel-Perspective-Seoul-ebook/dp/B01BAEVN7I	**8 Eyes on Korea, A Travel Perspective of Seoul, Korea** by Anna Lint (Author) James Lint (Author), Patrick Hughes (Foreword), Jim Watkins (Photographer), Antonio Rucci (Photographer), Kat Lysaght (Photographer)

Acknowledgements

I want to thank the many people who helped mold and build my skills. Some of the early ones have marched into the sunset and standing duty on a higher ground. I have many recent friends and guides above and below my grade. They all had lessons for me to learn. I am thankful for their assistance and guidance. I hope this book will provide support for the current Federal Government workers with quality new employees. I hope my friends who are currently working will guide and mentor the future new employees as well as others did for my career.

Thank you for the great graphic art support from: Sukyong Kim, Jee Sun Kim, and Dr. Soo Joon Lee.

James R. Lint

References

American Military University. Retrieved from http://www.amu.apus.edu/

AMU (October 3, 2013). How a Virtual Veterans Center supports military students. Retrieved from https://www.military1.com/college/article/406472-how-a-virtual-veterans-center-supports-military-students/

Anderson, D. (February 3, 2015). Harford community speaks out on possible job cuts at Aberdeen Proving Ground. Retrieved from http://www.baltimoresun.com/news/maryland/harford/abingdon/ph-ag-apg-listening-session-0204-20150130-story.html

Army Counterintelligence Discussion Group (ACIDG-L). Retrieved from https://groups.yahoo.com/neo/groups/ACIDG-L/info

Army Linguists. Retrieved from http://www.goarmy.com/linguist/language-programs.html

ASIS International. Retrieved from https://www.asisonline.org/About-ASIS/Pages/default.aspx

Association of Former Intelligence Officers. Retrieved from http://www.afio.com/01_about.htm

Berlitz Website. Retrieved from http://www.berlitz.us/

CIA Careers & Internships. Retrieved from https://www.cia.gov/careers/opportunities/analytical

Compendium of Published Works by James R. Lint. Retrieved from http://professor-lint.blogspot.com/2016/12/compendium-of-published-works-by-james.html

Create a USAJOBS Profile. Retrieved from https://www.usajobs.gov/

Data, Analysis & Documentation. Retrieved from https://www.opm.gov/policy-data-oversight/data-analysis-documentation/federal-employment-reports/historical-tables/total-government-employment-since-1962/

DEA Careers/Occupations. Retrieved from https://www.dea.gov/careers/occupations.shtml

DHS Careers. Retrieved from https://www.dhs.gov/homeland-security-careers

DIA Careers Foreign Languages. Retrieved from Dhttp://www.dia.mil/Careers/Foreign-Languages/

DLIFLC Employment. Retrieved from http://www.dliflc.edu/administration/employment/

FBI Jobs. Retrieved from https://www.fbijobs.gov/career-paths

Intelligence Careers. Retrieved from https://www.intelligencecareers.gov/

Intelligence Community Whistleblower Protection Act (ICWPA). Retrieved from http://www.dodig.mil/programs/whistleblower/icwpa.html

Intelligence Specialist (Operations). Retrieved from https://my.usajobs.gov/GetJob/ViewDetails/459437100

Learn about the Federal Application Process. Retrieved from https://www.usajobs.gov/?c=fed-app-process

Lint, J. (2013). Leadership and Management Lessons Learned. Amazon Digital Services LLC. Retrieved from https://www.amazon.com/Leadership-Management-Lessons-Learned-Vignettes-ebook/dp/B00G04EG1E

Marine Corps Counterintelligence Association. Retrieved from
http://mccia.org/Public/About/Benefits.aspx

Military Intelligence Corps Association. Retrieved from http://mica-national.org/about-us/

National Military Intelligence Association. Retrieved from
http://www.nmia.org/?AboutNMIA

Naval Intelligence Professionals. Retrieved from http://www.navintpro.org/

NSA Careers. Retrieved from
https://www.intelligencecareers.gov/nsa/nsacareers.html

OPSEC Professionals Society. Retrieved from http://opsecsociety.org/

Peace Corps Website. Retrieved from https://www.peacecorps.gov/

Pollicino, J. (June 9, 2013). PRISM whistleblower Edward Snowden reveals
himself, reasons for leaking surveillance program. Retrieved from
https://www.engadget.com/2013/06/09/prism-whistleblower-edward-snowden-reveals-himself-reasons/

Rossheim, J. (n.d.). Understand Recruitment Cycles to Give Your Job Search an
Edge. Retrieved from https://www.monster.com/career-advice/article/job-search-recruitment-cycles

Special Agent and Uniformed Division Pre-Employment Review (SUPER)
Interview Information. Retrieved from
https://www.secretservice.gov/join/apply/interview/

Stand with Snowden. Retrieved from https://standwithsnowden.com/

US Dept. of State Careers. Retrieved from
https://careers.state.gov/work/foreign-service/consular-fellows

VA History and Timeline. Retrieved from
http://www.benefits.va.gov/gibill/history.asp

Volkshochschule Website. Retrieved from
https://www.vhs.frankfurt.de/desktopdefault.aspx/tabid-295/526_read-2275/

We the People. Retrieved from https://petitions.whitehouse.gov/

What should I include in my federal resume? Retrieved from
https://www.usajobs.gov/Help/faq/application/documents/resume/what-to-include/

Yonsei University Website. Retrieved from http://www.yonsei.ac.kr/en_sc/

Made in the USA
Middletown, DE
24 October 2017